Bullyproof

A Teacher's Guide on Teasing and Bullying

For Use With Fourth and Fifth Grade Students

Developed by Nan Stein
Formulated by Nan Stein and Emily Gaberman
Written by Lisa Sjostrom and Nan Stein
Illustrated by Dominic Cappello
A joint publication of the Wellesley College Center for Research on Women and
the NEA Professional Library

Printing History
First Printing January 1996

Note: The opinions expressed in this publication do not necessarily represent the policy or position of the National Education Association. These materials are intended to be discussion documents for educators who are concerned with specialized interests of the profession.

NEA stock #1873-7-00-C4

ISBN 0-9641921-1-X

CRW 12

Bullyproof

Table of Contents

Preface v

Acknowledgments vi

Letter from a Teacher vii

Introduction 1

    Preparation 1
    Supplementary Materials.. 1
    Sequencing of Lessons 1
    Some Opening Notes on Teaching Style 1
    A Selection of Writing Options 3

Topical Cross-Reference of Activities 5

Core Lessons

    1. Teasing vs. Bullying: A Teacher-led Discussion (1-2 class sessions) 6
       Homework: "Crossing the Line," Writing Assignment 9

    2. On the Lookout: Student Observations (ongoing activity) 11
       Student Handout: "On the Lookout! Be a Researcher in School" 14
       Student Handout: "On the Lookout! Research Notes" 15

    3. Role Plays: Student Presentations and Analyses (2-3 class sessions) 16
       Homework: "Web of Courage," Writing Assignment 18

    4. Courage by Degrees: Evaluation and Discussion (1 class session) 20
       Homework: "Personal Principles," Writing Assignment 21

    5. Get the Picture: Cartoon Design and Discussion (1 class session) 22
       Student Handout: "Get the Picture" 23

    6. Sticks and Stones: Class Discussion and Webbing Activity (1-2 class sessions) 24
       Homework: "Tomboys and Sissies," Op-ed Piece and Interview 25
       Student Handout: "Sticks and Stones" 27

    7. Real Dilemmas: Case Studies and Class Discussion (2-6 class sessions) 29
       One Mother's Dilemma 32
       The Playground 34
       The Bus Ride 35
       Badgered By Boys 37
       Rites of Passage 39
       Mooing and More 41

8. What Are Your Rights? A Review and Discussion (1-2 class sessions) 43
   Student Handout: "Sexual Harassment: It's No Joke!" 45
   Teaching Notes: "Laws Regarding Sexual Harassment..." 46
   Teaching Notes: "Send a Letter to the Harasser/Bully" 47

9. Writing a Letter to A Harasser or Bully: A Review (1 class session) 49
   Homework: "In Plain Words," Writing Assignment 49
   Student Handout: "Sample Letter to the Harasser/Bully" 51

10. Action Alert! A Brainstorm and Action Planning (ongoing activity) 53

11. Letter to a Friend: In-class Writing Assignment and Discussion (1 class session) ... 55

Resources 57

   Books, Handbooks, and Articles on Bullying 57
   Miscellaneous Resources on Bullying 58
   Articles on Sexual Harassment 58
   Reports, Guides, and Pamphlets on Sexual Harassment 59
   Books for Children 59
   Organizations Working for Equity in Schools 60

Preface

Bullying is part of the evaded curriculum* in school—we all know it's there but we rarely talk about it in a sustained, non-judgmental, age-appropriate manner. Very young children can tell us what the word means. Many of them have been bullied even before they arrive at the schoolyard gate. And most children, even those who haven't been explicitly targeted by a bully, have witnessed bullying in action.

Bullying remains an under-studied phenomenon in the United States, in contrast with Britain, Norway and Sweden.** When bullying has been acknowledged, studies have focused on the pathology of the bully instead of the whole school culture; or bullying has been regarded as an unfortunate stage that some children go through on their way to adolescence and adulthood. Attention has too rarely been given to the witnesses, bystanders and observers of bullying, those children who are neither targeters nor perpetrators, yet who are also affected by the phenomena of bullying in school.

Regardless of how the problem has been framed, we have been bereft of classroom lessons on bullying—until now. **Bullyproof** contains eleven sequential core lessons comprised of writing activities, reading assignments, class discussions, role plays, case studies and homework assignments that engage children to think about the distinctions between "teasing" and "bullying." These activities help children focus on the boundaries between appropriate and inappropriate, playful and hurtful behavior. During the piloting of these lessons, children gained a conceptual framework and a common vocabulary that allowed them to find their own links between teasing and bullying, and eventually sexual harassment.***

Bullying, like its older cousin sexual harassment, needs to be addressed as a matter of social justice: it is an affront to democracy and our democratic institutions. Bullying deprives children of their rightful entitlement to go to school in a safe, just and caring environment; bullying interferes with children's learning, concentration, and desire to go to school. Bullying may not be "illegal" in the same manner as sexual harassment, but it may in fact be the fertile practice field for sexual harassment behaviors. Whether or not the antecedents of peer sexual harassment in school lie in bullying, its existence in schools deserves our attention and concern. We must name, study, and discuss bullying in a deliberate manner with all children, not just with the bully or his/her targets.

---

* Wellesley College Center for Research on Women, *The AAUW Report: How Schools Shortchange Girls* (Washington, D.C., The American Association of University Women Educational Foundation, 1992), pp. 75-82.

** C. Keise, *Sugar and Spice? Bullying in Single-Sex Schools* (Staffordshire, England: Trentham Books, 1992); D. Olweus, *Bullying At School: What We Know and What We Can Do* (Oxford: Blackwell, 1993); I. Whitney and P.K. Smith, "A Survey of the Nature and Extent of Bullying in the Junior/Middle and Secondary Schools," *Educational Research* 35, no 1; and several publications by and/or edited by Delwyn Tattum at the Countering Bullying Unit, Professional Development Centre, Cardiff Institute of Higher Education, Cardiff, Wales, UK. Also see H. Claire, *We Can Stop It! Whole School Approaches to Combat Bullying*: A Handbook for Teachers (London, England: Islington Education Department, 1991)

*** Nan Stein, "Sexual Harassment in K-12 Schools: The Public Performance of Gendered Violence," *Harvard Educational Review* 65, no.2 (Summer 1995), pp. 145-162.

Acknowledgments

During the Clarence Thomas/Anita Hill hearings in October 1991, I was in Washington D.C. with my eight-year-old niece Rebecca. All I wanted to do was watch the hearings, but how was I to interest a child in them? Somehow, Rebecca and I hit upon the concept of "bullying"; I began explaining sexual harassment in terms she understood, and she provided me with a catalog of examples of bullying in her school.

Since 1979 I have been working to create strategies for teachers and administrators to prevent peer-to-peer sexual harassment in middle and high schools. Thanks to Rebecca, I became even more interested in working with younger children and their teachers on the subject of teasing and bullying as the antecedents of sexual harassment. In late 1992 I received support from The Patrina Foundation, a private foundation in New York, to conduct a pilot project involving seven classrooms in three elementary schools in Boston and Brookline, MA.

In 1995, a generous gift for the curriculum development portion of this project came from Phyllis Henderson Carey, Wellesley Class of 1946, in memory of her daughter-in-law Julie A. Baucom. Early support for the production phase of the curriculum came from Carla Wengren Ricci. Their support allowed me to team up with the talented writer Lisa Sjostrom, who is once again my co-author on a project.

Original art work and illustrations are by Dominic Cappello, Seattle-based educator, writer, cartoonist and long-time friend. In exchange for my comments on his latest educational production, *Life Lessons*, Dominic generously agreed to create cartoons for **Bullyproof**. I am indebted to seven teachers, one guidance counselor, and three principals: from the Agassiz School in Boston, principal Alfredo Nunez and three fourth grade teachers, Grace Madsen, Susan Switalski, and Grace Donahue; from the Runkle School in Brookline, principal Dr. Marty Sleeper and three fifth grade teachers, Emily Gaberman, Deanne Dixon and Nancy Springer; and from the Driscoll School in Brookline, principal Carol Schraft, guidance counselor Wallis Raemer, and two fifth grade teachers, Marc Lofchie and Sandy Levi. I worked with these fourth and fifth grade teachers and their students for one year at the Agassiz and Driscoll Schools and for more than two years at the Runkle School. At every juncture, all of these teachers generously gave of their time and experience, helping me to formulate age-appropriate lessons, discussions, and assignments, even editing in real time the words that I used when speaking with their students. During the summer of 1993, Emily Gaberman of the Runkle School worked on synthesizing, organizing and consolidating the words of the children from all seven classrooms into a more cohesive unit. Emily also created several of the activities and assignments (word splash and "principles"), and has my gratitude for introducing me to the book *Bridge to Terabithia* which later became a important piece of this curriculum unit.

Finally, I find myself again indebted to a child for naming one of my curriculum projects. Nora Wiske Dillon of the Runkle School came up with the title, **Bullyproof**, that seemed to best capture the spirit of this project. Thank you, Nora. I wish I had room to thank every child from all the classes who contributed to this project.

Nan Stein, November 1995

Letter from a Teacher

Dear Fellow Teachers, **Bullyproof** has helped to build community in my fifth grade classroom. The first year I taught the curriculum, my students were grappling with the social dynamics and undercurrents typical among ten-year-olds. More specifically, new students were being excluded by others. As we progressed through the lessons and broadened the definitions of teasing and bullying to include a wide range of behaviors, students became sensitized to each other's feelings and learned to empathize with one another. Students became more conscious of themselves and how they were perceived by others. They began reflecting upon their own attitudes and behaviors. Eventually, they were able to address the sensitive issue of inclusion and exclusion head on.

Several questions deserve consideration before you begin to teach **Bullyproof**. First, where should you place the curriculum in the sequence of other related or non-related units? My experience over the past three years suggests that mid-way through the school year is the best time to teach the lessons. Of course, it is important to teach **Bullyproof** early enough in the year so that you and your students can reap the benefits of establishing a safe learning environment for all. But these lessons also call for a level of trust and honesty among students that is not always inherent at the start of the year. Use your own best judgement when determining timing.

What is an appropriate pacing of the lessons? When Nan first came to our school to pilot **Bullyproof**, the project extended over an eight week period. In subsequent years, I have found that it works well to devote as many as two or three sessions a week to **Bullyproof**, as time allows. It's best to follow the natural flow of your own classroom as the lessons progress.

Could **Bullyproof** be led by a third party in the school, such as a guidance counselor, rather than by the classroom teacher? If it is possible, I recommend co-teaching **Bullyproof** with a "disinterested" person who can lead the discussions in close collaboration with you, the classroom teacher who knows the students best.

My students' final assignments perhaps speak loudest of **Bullyproof**'s effectiveness (see page 56). After completing the lessons, most students perceived some positive difference in either themselves, the class, or both. Students wrote of the value of putting oneself in another's shoes, describing this as an effective method for creating empathy for target, bystander, and bully alike.

Bullyproof provided my students with a platform and a common vocabulary for discussing how to treat one another fairly in the classroom and on the playground. I think these lessons are an excellent way to establish an individual's responsibility to the group and to both promote and practice the ideal of a shared classroom community.

Sincerely,

Emily Gaberman

Emily Gaberman
Fifth Grade Teacher
Runkle School
Brookline, MA

Introduction: Don't Skip This Section

Preparation

Before you begin, utilize the appropriate steps that your district has designated to introduce a new curriculum. Then read through **Bullyproof** in its entirety and tailor a program to suit other subject areas taught and particular time constraints faced in your classroom. You may also want to prepare journals and/or folders in which students can record their thoughts and collect handouts and homework.

Supplementary Materials

We strongly recommend that you order one supplementary material, *Tune In To Your Rights: A Guide for Teenagers About Turning Off Sexual Harassment*, to use in conjunction with Lesson 7 of **Bullyproof**. *Tune In To Your Rights*, which has been printed in English, Spanish and Arabic, is available for $4.00 from Programs for Educational Opportunity, School of Education, #1005, University of Michigan, Ann Arbor, MI 48109-1259, or you can call (313) 763-9910 to place an order for your classroom. You might also contact individuals who work in your state's Office of Educational Opportunity; they might have sets of this guide on hand which are available for loan—or they might help your school district purchase a classroom set.

We also suggest reinforcing and expanding upon **Bullyproof** with Katherine Paterson's *Bridge To Terabithia* (1977). The two main characters in the novel, a 5th grade girl and boy, have to decide how to deal with the school bully. Since the story reveals that the bully is a victim of child abuse, the novel provides students with an avenue for talking about possible underlying causes of bullying. One caveat: the story relays a second, if unintended, message that it is dangerous, even life-threatening, to be an unconventional girl. Be sure to scrutinize and carefully assess the implications of this message with your students.

Sequencing of Lessons

The **Bullyproof** lessons follow in a purposeful sequential order. All of the main lessons should be included in the unit and, though most effectively taught over consecutive days, the lessons may be spread out over a number of weeks. Freely tailor lessons to suit your own classroom and time frame. For example, you may want to augment a case study with a writing exercise, devote extra time to a particular discussion, or create a homework assignment of your own.

Some Opening Notes on Teaching Style

The issues of teasing and bullying are emotionally charged and personal in nature. It is important to create as safe a space as possible for students to honestly discuss their experiences, opinions and feelings. The following points are suggested as ways to help create a safe environment.

Respect. It is important for teachers to model respectful behavior. It is crucial to take seriously and be sensitive to students' individual differences and perspectives, as well as any discomfort students experience during discussions of teasing and bullying incidents. If students become defensive, start acting out, or giggling, take time to talk with them about what they find difficult.

Judgment. Be careful not to make judgments or incriminations. Beware not to reinforce stereotypes, for example, that "boys will be boys" or that girls are powerless "victims." Keep the focus on the facts.

Disclosure. You should think through beforehand strategies for dealing with any instances of abuse and neglect that may be evoked by these lessons or disclosed during discussions. Sometimes a student simply needs someone to listen. Sometimes you may need to refer students to the school psychologist or counselor. Be sure to follow the reporting procedures required by your state law and school district policy.

Safety and Ground Rules. Ask the students themselves what they need from you and from each other in order to feel safe talking about teasing and bullying. For example, do they need the right to refuse to participate? To foster open discussion, lay down ground rules before you begin *each* exercise. For example, before a discussion students can be reminded that everyone's input matters; to listen to one another without interrupting; and to talk about actual people and situations without mentioning specific names.

If discussion becomes heated, remind students that there are ways to disagree respectfully without resorting to name calling or insults. To refocus the class, you can ask students to put their thoughts down in writing (see "A Selection of Writing Options").

Another way to create safety for students is to set up a "question box" in which students can anonymously pose questions which might be difficult to raise in front of peers. Ask students to indicate whether or not they want their questions to be read aloud. If so, you can answer questions in class without reference to individuals. If not, you can talk with students individually.

Diversity. When dividing students for group exercises, aim to create groups which mix the students by sex, race and ethnic background, socio-economic status, and popularity. Be sure to integrate any special education students and/or children with disabilities among the groups too. Students may initially feel more comfortable or say that they want to be in select groups, but one of the goals of this project is to open communication across diverse lines.

Language. The language you establish for class discussions will help determine the attitudes students take away from the lessons. In particular, avoid using the word "victim" when describing the "target" of a bully. Targets are not powerless, whereas the word "victim" often implies a kind of powerlessness. This guide provides numerous examples of actions both targets and bystanders can take in response to teasing or bullying incidents.

Use both pronouns "he" and "she" when referring to targets of teasing or bullying.

Many of the teasing and bullying behaviors and scenarios described in this curriculum can be seen and legally defined as sexual harassment. When teaching young students, however, it is more useful and age-appropriate to discuss these behaviors within the framework of teasing and bullying, concepts already familiar to children, using words that are most likely a working part of students' vocabulary.

If you see what you consider to be an incident of student-to-student sexual harassment in school, one of the most effective ways to stop the behavior is to say, "This is inappropriate behavior for school. That's not allowed here." It is not wise to label the behavior "sexual harassment" because, given the subjective definition of sexual harassment, students might respond to you by saying, "We both like this, it's mutual." For similar reasons, avoid the response, "That offends me!"

Fourth and fifth grade students may not initially identify with the term "sexual harassment." Using the term "bullying" or "sexual bullying" with younger students may make sexual harassment easier to understand.

Illustrations. The cartoons appearing on the handouts throughout this guide have been deliberately drawn so that students themselves can add shading and color.

A Selection of Writing Options

Vocabulary Wordsplash. Before beginning **Bullyproof**, cull words from the lessons onto a vocabulary list for your students to define and refer to throughout the unit. One creative way to familiarize students with new words is to "splash" or randomly write five to ten words related to a lesson on the board. Ask students to choose pairs of words that they think are related and to explain the words' relationship to the class. Draw a line between the two words and note the relationship (synonyms, antonyms, cause and effect, nouns, verbs, etc.) on the line. Draw from the following list of words and add more of your own:

> ally, animosity, badger, bother, buddy, bully, bystander, conform, courage, dilemma, double standard, embarrass, empathy, escalate, exclude, fight, friend, harass, include, intervene, intimidate, jeer, negotiate, offend, popular, principle, reconcile, respect, scapegoat, sexism, sissy, target, taunt, tease, tomboy, tradition, unpopular, witness, wuss

Homework Assignments. In-class and homework writing assignments have been built directly into most of the lessons in this guide. Students often produce better work when they are encouraged to submit first drafts of an assignment (i.e., in which spelling errors "don't count") and then given the opportunity to refine their work in a second draft.

Freewriting. Along with the writing assignments mapped out in this guide, feel free to weave spontaneous journal and "freewriting" exercises into classes at any point. The following options are particularly effective when class discussion and dynamics become heated, complicated or difficult; or when particular students become defensive or overbearing. At such moments, student writing may serve to "democratize" the class discussion. Putting pen to paper gives students the chance to regain composure, collect thoughts, and safely express feelings and opinions that might get lost in the larger or louder discussion. After the freewrite, return to discussion by asking students to take turns reading their freewrites aloud with their nearest neighbor, or by asking for student volunteers to read their writing aloud to the class.

Freewrites in the Midst of Class Discussions: At any point during discussion, ask students to write a response to one of the following questions:
- What would you like to add to this conversation right now?
- What do you think of "Sam's" point? Write him a short letter explaining your ideas.
- Do you agree or disagree with what "Anna" just said? Why?

Freewrites After Case Studies, Role Plays, or Discussion of a Bullying Incident: After concluding discussion of a case or incident, ask students to write one of the following options:
- Write a diary entry or interior monologue in the voice of the target, bystander or bully: "Put yourself in his/her shoes and tell what's happening, what you are thinking, and how you feel at this moment." (Assign portions of the class different roles to explore.)
- Same as above with an added stipulation: each writing should end with the statement, "I don't know what to do." (As students read their freewrites aloud, ask the rest of the class to brainstorm solutions. Or, ask students to swap papers with a neighbor and respond in writing on the same page. Ask for volunteers to read aloud their entries and responses to the class.)
- Add yourself to the scene as a third party bystander: "If you *saw* this happening, what would you do?" (Ask students to write their own conclusions to the scene with themselves playing critical roles.)
- Assume the role of an older/younger sibling of the character being bullied in the case and write down a dinner table conversation which involves discussion of the incident.
- Write a hypothetical dialogue between two people (already in the scene or whom you create); for example:

1. A conversation about the incident between two bystanders.
2. A conversation between a parent and child who is a target of a bully.
3. An interchange/conversation between the target and the bully.
4. An interchange/conversation between a bystander and the bully.

- Write a "dialogue poem" from the paired perspectives of two people involved in the situation. The poem consists of a number of two-line stanzas; the first line is written from one person's point of view, the second from another's. For example, you might compare the thoughts of a bully and a target:

> Time to go to school.
> *Can't I stay home, dad – my stomach hurts.*
>
> Bus is late again!
> *I hope the driver got lost.*
>
> Let's see if I can make him cry.
> *Why me?...*

Freewrites or Homework in Response to a Comment, Quotation, Question or Fact: Any provocative word or line from a case study, article or discussion can be a springboard or "prompt" into writing. Write the prompt on the board and ask students to try one of the following options:
- Use the prompt as the starting point of a poem.
- Write a letter in which you expand upon or agree/disagree with the prompt.
- Write a short story in which the prompt appears at any point.

Examples of possible writing prompts:

- "Boys will be boys."
- "Can't you take a joke?"
- "What part of 'No' don't you understand?!"
- "Be a buddy, not a bully."

Topical Cross-Reference of Activities

General Topic	Activity
Perception of Social Norms	Teasing vs. Bullying; On the Lookout; Courage By Degrees; Sticks and Stones; Tomboys and Sissies
Perception of Teasing/Bullying	Teasing vs. Bullying; Crossing the Line; On the Lookout; Courage By Degrees
Strategies to Prevent Teasing/Bullying	Role Plays; Web of Courage; Courage By Degrees; Personal Principles; Sticks and Stones; Real Dilemmas; What are Your Rights?; Letter to a Friend
Responses to Teasing/Bullying: Target	Crossing the Line; Role Plays; Web of Courage; Courage By Degrees; Personal Principles; Real Dilemmas; What Are Your Rights?; Letter to a Harasser or Bully; Letter to a Friend
Responses to Teasing/Bullying: Bystanders	On the Lookout; Role Plays; Web of Courage; Courage By Degrees; Personal Principles; Sticks and Stones; Real Dilemmas; Letter to a Friend
Definition of Sexual Harassment	Real Dilemmas; What are Your Rights?
Information about Legal Rights	Real Dilemmas; What Are Your Rights?
Strategies to Prevent Sexual Harassment	What Are Your Rights?; Letter to a Harasser or Bully

Lesson 1. Teasing vs. Bullying
A Teacher-led Discussion
(1-2 class sessions)

Objectives

To raise student awareness of the kinds of joking, teasing and bullying which regularly take place; to discern the subjective line between these categories; to encourage appropriate interventions in teasing and bullying incidents; to make public a social problem that interferes with student learning, cooperation, concentration and self-esteem; to promote open student discussion of a complicated topic.

Teaching Note

During this activity, students may mention examples of behavior that you think qualify as sexual harassment. If this happens, let the students decide where on the lists these examples belong. This is not the time for teachers to introduce the terms "sexual harassment" or "sexist" to the discussion—**unless** a student raises these concepts and words himself or herself. Sexism and sexual harassment will be introduced and discussed in later lessons.

Preparation

• Prepare three lists with headings and subheadings on either the chalkboard or on big sheets of newsprint (these sheets may be used as references in later lessons). Title the three lists "Words," "Gestures," and "Physical." Under each main heading, write the three subheadings "Joking," "Teasing" and "Bullying." During the discussion, anticipate creating a fourth subheading at the bottom of each of the three lists titled "It Depends..." At this point, the three lists should look like this:

Words
Joking Teasing Bullying

Gestures
Joking Teasing Bullying

Physical
Joking Teasing Bullying

• *Important Note:* Your students may want to elaborate upon the subheadings "teasing" and "bullying" to include additional categories of behavior. During the piloting of this lesson, some students indicated that a third category, "fooling around/joking," precedes teasing and that a fourth category, "Fighting/Violence," may follow bullying. Allow enough space on the three lists for additional subheadings—as students indicate.

• Decide beforehand if you will allow students to use profanity and "bad words" during the activity or if they should speak in euphemisms. An alternative is for students to write their answers on small pieces of paper or note cards and hand these to you to decide later what to record on the lists.

• Ask students to arrange their chairs in a circle or semi-circle, if possible.

• Decide upon the ground rules; e.g.,

1) Everyone must listen when someone is speaking.
2) Don't get personal by mentioning anyone's name when telling about a specific incident.
3) Ask students to determine other guidelines.

• Encourage students to be in their most "mature" behavior mode.

Introduction

"This activity is simple and fun. We're going to talk about the differences between joking, teasing, and bullying. Before we begin, I want to emphasize that we're not here to blame or change anyone in particular. Some of us have been teased and bullied, some of us have teased and bullied others, and some of us have been in both positions. But *all* of us are observers and bystanders who see teasing and bullying happen during the day in school, on the playground, on the school bus and in other places, and we all need to learn to say, 'Knock it off, that's not funny!,' or 'Hey, what if that were your sister or little brother?' So we're here to develop courage in *all* of us—courage to actively respond when we see someone being teased or bullied.

"Each of you is an expert on teasing and bullying—and on human behavior. Every day you see and hear how kids treat each other, and you know how behaviors differ depending on where you are, who you are, and whether or not adults are around. So, in this discussion, I want you to draw upon what you already know from your own experiences and observations in school—in class, on the playground, in the cafeteria, at special events—as we try to make sense between what is just fooling around, what is teasing and what is bullying.

"First we'll focus on the words people say or write, such as comments and notes. Then we'll focus on gestures like winking, waving and other ways we communicate through movement without talking or touching. Last, we'll consider interactions which involve physical contact between people. For each category, we'll talk about examples of joking and fooling around, and examples which cross the line into teasing and into bullying.

"I don't expect everyone to agree, but I do expect everyone to listen. What's most important is that we start talking together. Can anyone give me an example of a comment someone says when joking and fooling around?..."

Activity

- To avoid confusion, walk students through the lists one at a time.

- Write down student answers under the appropriate subheading.

- Encourage students to stay with specifics they know from actual incidents in school and not to stray to hypothetical situations.

- If one column isn't being addressed, ask students specific questions; e.g., "Can anyone think of a time teasing included physical contact between people?"

- When students disagree about where words or a behavior belong on a list, ask them to explain the criteria upon which they are basing their opinion. For example, perhaps the nature of a comment depends upon whether or not the speaker is a friend, or upon the speaker's tone of voice. Enter these dependent variables under the additional heading "It Depends" on the appropriate list.

- If an example falls under both headings of "Joking" and "Teasing" or of "Teasing" and "Bullying," note this by drawing an arrow from one column to the other; e.g.:

Words

Joking	Teasing	Bullying	Violence
	You got big ears	nerd	
	flat-chested	when you say something about someone they can't change	
	four eyes		
	Not letting someone join because of how they look ⟶		
	toothpick	racial slurs	
	motor mouth	faggot	
	you dummy	chicken	
	your mother ⟶		
	fatso ⟶		
	teased you are weak ⟶	when you don't want to fight back	

It Depends
is s/he smiling or laughing?
body language
tone of voice

Gestures

Joking	Teasing	Bullying	Violence
	middle finger ⟶		
	sticking out tongue	stealing something	
	mimicking someone's walk ⟶		
	making faces	being framed	
	sticking finger in mouth	shooting spitballs	
	cheerio sign, "O"	sucking your teeth	
	whistling ⟶		
	buck teeth	pretending to be crazy	
	knocking head against desk	hitting fist in palm	
	snapping fingers ⟶		
	rolling eyes		
	burping in someone's face		

It Depends
who else is around
if s/he is your friend

Physical

Joking	Teasing	Bullying	Violence
	hiding	punching	
	picked last	head lock	
	mock kick	kicking	
	pulling hair or ear	slamming or slapping	
	pushing ⟶		
	patting back	poke eyes	
	mimic a kick	slapping back of head	
	"play" fight	body slam	
	stealing glasses ⟶	then called four-eyes	
		no one plays with you	
		"noogie"	
		tackling	

It Depends
playing a joke on oneself
do both people like the behavior?

Questions to Raise Afterwards

The following discussion questions can help students begin to make sense of the lists:

1. What is a bully?
2. What does a bully's presence feel like? How can you tell when a bully's around?
3. What are some common forms of teasing and bullying that often go unnoticed in school?
4. If bullying hurts people, how come it goes on?
5. Do teasing and bullying have any affect on your schoolwork?
6. Are there behaviors that come before "joking"? What would you call this category?
7. What behaviors come after "bullying"?
8. How do you decide if something is joking or teasing? Teasing or bullying?

Troubleshooting

Discussion often gets heated and complicated. You may need to intervene and troubleshoot at various points. Here are some typical scenarios, along with suggested responses:

1) Students interrupt one another, everyone begins talking and disagreeing at once.
   "We all have to be in the same conversation, so we all have to listen. We don't all have to agree. It's good to travel through a lot of opinions and disagreements because this is a personal subject for everyone."

2) Students feel uncomfortable due to some of the language and examples used in the discussion.
   "Yes, these words and examples *should* make you feel uncomfortable—because that's exactly what teasing and bullying do."

3) Students disagree over examples due to different cultural norms and expectations.
   "We all bring different—and valid—opinions and perspectives to this discussion. Sometimes the words we say and the things we do have different meanings to different people. Each of us decides what is and isn't okay behavior based on our family upbringing, ethnic background, religious beliefs, etc. If you were raised in the Buddhist religion, for example, you might consider it a grave insult if I patted the top of your head because that is where Buddhists believe that the soul resides. So we need to listen to one another carefully and understand that the same word or gesture might mean different things depending on where you're coming from.

4) A student calls an incident "sexual harassment."
   "Sometimes you are bullied or harassed *because* of your particular sex: because you are a girl or because you are a boy. For example, boys can be teased about certain body parts and girls can be teased about others. Such behavior is inappropriate for school and, just like bullying, can make you feel threatened, afraid, humiliated, angry, and sometimes trapped. This form of teasing and bullying is called sexual harassment. Sexual harassment is serious and illegal, and it is the school's responsibility to make sure that it doesn't go on here. If you are being sexually bullied or harassed, it is very important to talk to an adult you trust so that steps can be taken to end the behavior."

Homework
Crossing the Line: A Short Story

(writing assignment)

Objectives

To discern the line between fooling around and teasing or bullying, as well as the intentions and feelings of people involved; to introduce the responsibility of bystanders.

Teaching Note

After students have submitted their homework assignments, select and set aside several of the most representative stories to serve as role plays in Lesson 3.

Assignment

"Can you think about a time when joking around and teasing went too far and crossed the line into bullying?"

Ask students to write a short story or a journal entry about a situation where fooling around went too far. Instruct them to try to base their story on an incident they have experienced themselves or have actually seen—using false names. Suggest the following guidelines:

- Feel free to draw upon the lists created in the "Teasing vs. Bullying" activity.
- Characters can be any age and either sex.
- Include descriptions: where and when the situation is happening, characters' (false) names, their appearance, and so on.
- Include characters' dialogue, thoughts and feelings.
- Since both joking around, teasing and bullying often happen in public, include other people who see what is happening.

Debriefing: A Teacher-led Discussion

- After students have handed in and you have reviewed their homework, choose several stories to read aloud to the class. Ask students if they'd

prefer you to read the stories without identifying the authors or if they'd like to read aloud their own. Possible discussion questions for the class:

1. Is this fooling around, teasing or bullying? How can you tell?
2. What should s/he do now? (If students are stumped, lay out options to choose from: ignore him/her? say something? fight back? tell a friend?)
3. What are the best ways to handle a bully? What have you tried?
4. If you were standing nearby and saw this happen, what would you do?

- This debriefing period can also serve as a test-run for the role plays which follow in Lesson 3. During the discussion, ask students to improvise on the spur-of-the-moment as either targets or bystanders. **Do not permit students to serve in the role of either a bully or a harasser**; it's critical not to place students in situations where they might intimidate, scare or injure one another. Instead, the *teacher* can enact a modi-fied version of the bully part (i.e., expunge all pushing or shoving) or read aloud the role of the bully during the improvisation.

- During the impromptu role play, ask students what they could say or do to get the bully to stop; students get the chance to "try on" and see one another taking proactive stances against bullies.

Lesson 2.
On the Lookout
Student Observations
(over several days or a week)

Objectives

To encourage students to be researchers in their school; to raise awareness of the prevalence of teasing and bullying; to assess the roles of targets and bystanders.

Preparation

- Photocopy and distribute the following handout "On the Lookout!" (p. 14), and the form for students "Research Notes" (p. 15).
- If students will record research notes on index cards or in "blue books," rather than on the form, distribute these to the class.

Background Teaching Note (don't read aloud!)

In this activity, students are asked to be researchers within their own school culture; in fact, they are assuming the role of ethnographers. Ethnography is a type of qualitative research that attempts to describe a culture or aspects of a culture. Sometimes referred to as "thick description," ethnography is a sister science of anthropology. Ethnographic research is rich in description of people, places and conversations; and data is collected in the field, in the setting where subjects normally spend their time, as opposed to laboratories or other researcher-controlled sites. An ethnographer begins a study as a cultural "outsider" and attempts to view the culture from the frame of reference of the people studied. Through the keeping of a detailed record of what s/he hears and observes, an ethnographer eventually begins to possess an

"insider's" view. Ethnographers are interested not only in people's behavior, but also in the shared meanings people attribute to events within a culture (e.g., the various meanings of a wink of an eye, or the raising of hands in a classroom).*

Introduction

- Ask students to name areas in the school known to "belong" to certain groups; for example, the area outside the boys' or girls' bathrooms, a certain section of the lunchroom, the gym, the playground, the parking lot, certain stairwells, etc. Compile a list on the board.

  "You know more about human behavior in this school than anyone else. You're experts on what really goes on here. You observe students and teachers day in and day out. You know how students' words and actions differ depending on where they are and whether or not there are adults nearby. So, you're in a great position to be researchers."

- Read aloud the handout "On the Lookout!" with students and explain that over the next few days (or weeks) they are to assume the role of researchers and observe the way students treat each other in school. They should focus on students' language, gestures and physical interactions. Ask the class to take special note of times where behavior or language "crosses the line" from joking into hurtful teasing and bullying.

---

* The "Background Note" on ethnography is taken from *Qualitative Research for Education*, by Robert C. Bogden and Sari Knopp Biklen (Allyn and Bacon, Needham Heights, MA, 1982).

Practice Run

- Before formally sending students out as researchers, guide them through simple test-runs for practice. Assign the entire class one or two pre-determined areas and behaviors to watch for during the day; for example:

  "When you go to lunch today, notice who sits with whom... At recess, notice who's hanging out together and what different groups of kids are doing. I'm going to visit you in the lunchroom and on the playground to see what you're discovering."

- Ask students to record their observations on the "Research Notes" form. They should note the day, time, and place where they witness a teasing or bullying incident, along with a description of the incident itself.

- Instruct students not to identify people by name, but instead to speak in generalizations; e.g., "3rd grade girls," "two older boys," etc. If possible, check in with students "on site" to confirm that they are proceeding correctly.

- After students have completed these initial practice runs during the school day, assign one additional observation for homework. Insert writing into the activity at this point:

  "Tomorrow morning when you're on the bus or walking to school, and then hanging around before entering the building, notice what's going on. Are some girls braiding each other's hair? Are kids doing homework, swapping clothes, telling jokes, playing together? Is anyone being teased or hurt? Write down in your research notes when and where behaviors are taking place; what you see and hear; and who is involved—older or younger kids, boys or girls—without using names."

- The next day during class, ask students to read through their forms and discuss their practice-run observations—*before* undertaking the major "On the Lookout" assignment.

Assignment

- Ask or assign students (or student teams) to "cover" one specific place or hangout, or the whole school, for the next few days. They should remain on the lookout for behaviors that cross the line from joking or fooling around into teasing or bullying.

- Review again the "On the Lookout!" handout and ask students if they have any questions.

- Remind students to jot down their observational notes (on the "Research Notes" forms, on index cards, or in blue books) as inconspicuously as possible without identifying people by name.

- Encourage students to observe the behavior of younger children in school as well as their peers.

- Assure students that the point of this activity is not to "snitch," "rat," "tattle" or inform on one another. Rather, they are taking on the role of reporters to gather information which can be used to raise awareness of the world in which they are all participating daily.

- Encourage students to see themselves as activists as well as reporters. Tell students that noting cruel, hurtful and unfair behavior is crucial, but only a first step. Behavior which is wrong calls out to be righted—through action. Inform students that after being "on the lookout" they will review the actions both kids and grown-ups can take to make the school a safer and fairer place.

Debriefing and Discussion

- You may set aside one specific time to discuss students' observations, or ask students to "check in" for several minutes at the start or the end of each class. Students may be surprised to realize how often, and on a continual basis, "lines get crossed."

- Ask students to report on their observations, without identifying names, in either a teacher-led discussion or with one another in small groups (in which case, discussion questions may be written on the board or handed out for the students to ask one another).

- To help students make sense of their observations, ask student pairs to analyze their research data and answer the following questions in a general class discussion.

- *Important Notes:* Please formulate your own questions concerning factors of race, social class, disability, immigrant status, etc., using examples and language that are both pertinent and familiar to students. Also, direct student attention to the importance of "bystanders" and discuss the different ways bystanders can influence a situation depending on whether and how they choose to respond (i.e., some bystanders help to de-escalate a conflict by speaking out against bullies; others collude by laughing).

Possible Discussion Questions

1. Where and when do teasing and bullying happen?
2. Who gets teased and bullied in school, and why?
3. What kinds of things do kids pick on the most?
4. Was popularity a factor?
5. Who bullies? Is there a typical profile?
6. When are fights most likely to break out? Why?
7. Were other people around when these incidents happened? How did they respond?
8. Did anyone try to stop the teasing or bullying? What happened, or why not?
9. Are all "bystanders" alike?
10. What is being "said," in a sense, when people don't speak up and intervene while someone is being teased or bullied?
11. How did *you* feel as a bystander?
12. What did you do in response, or could you do, if you saw this again next week?
13. What are three things the school can do to help stop teasing and bullying?

Optional Activity

- A symbolic picture. Ask students to draw a symbolic picture of what bullying feels or looks like. You may give students the option of drawing with their "wrong" hand in order to relieve the pressure to make a "accurate" representation.

ON THE LOOKOUT!
BE A RESEARCHER IN SCHOOL

Some researchers travel to Egypt to interpret hieroglyphics. Others journey to Montana to unearth minerals and mines. Some piece together dinosaur bones, while others scour libraries to find just the right book. But researchers don't only study dead or ancient artifacts. Researchers are just as fascinated by living places and people—sometimes girls and boys just like you!

So it isn't necessary to go far away to be on the lookout. You can research what happens in a living room, at an amusement park, on any city block. All that's needed to be a researcher is an open pair of eyes and ears, a pad and a pencil, and a good set of questions. These questions help you see things that have been in front of you all along, but which you might not have really noticed before.

Be on the lookout for the ways students treat one another in school: in your classes, in the hallways, during lunch period, on the playground, and on the bus. What do you see? What do you hear? Before you start taking notes, read the following tips and starting questions. Then add questions of your own on the back of the page.

Research Tips:

- Decide where you will observe: one particular place or many.
- Decide if you will work on your own, or with a partner or team.
- Watch for instances where words, gestures or physical interactions cross the line from teasing into bullying.
- Jot down observations as inconspicuously as possible.
- Write down the setting (day, time, place), as well as the behavior you see, what you hear, who is involved, and the reactions of anyone else nearby.
- Don't mention names. Instead, refer to people generally, such as "a 4th grade girl" or "2nd grade boy."
- Watch both younger and older students in school.

Keep on the Lookout:

- Are there any areas of the school that "belong" to bullies?
- What goes on between students that makes you uncomfortable, worried or angry?
- Where, when, and how do words and actions cross the line from teasing into bullying? How can you tell a line is being crossed?
- What kinds of words and drawings do you see on desks and bathroom walls?
- Who gets bullied?
- Does popularity have anything to do with bullying?
- How do people react when they are teased or bullied?

ON THE LOOKOUT!
RESEARCH NOTES

Day: _____   Time: _____

Place: _____

Observation:

Day: _____   Time: _____

Place: _____

Observation:

Day: _____   Time: _____

Place: _____

Observation:

Lesson 3. Role Plays
(2-3 class sessions)

Objectives

To try on roles and respond from the perspectives of the various people involved in bullying incidents; to understand the responsibilities of targets and bystanders; to critically evaluate intervention options.

Teaching Notes

Anticipate that the issues of "popularity" and "courage" will arise when students are grappling with intervention strategies. The relative popularity or unpopularity of the bully, the target and the intervenor profoundly figure into the equation of courage and intervention. It's easier for children to be courageous when a bully targets a popular student; it is more difficult to take a stand when a bully is your friend or targets an unpopular child. "Popularity" is specifically addressed in the discussion questions during the second class period devoted to role plays. "Courage" is specifically addressed during both the first and the second class periods, and in Lesson 4, "Courage by Degrees."

Preparation

- Student writings will serve as the basis for role plays. Preview and select the most representative stories from the "Crossing the Line" homework assignment. Assure that there is no possible way for students to identify the authors of the stories by their handwriting; it is best if you can type each scenario on a separate page.

- An entire story may constitute a role play; sometimes role plays can be one- or two-sentence excerpts from a long or complicated story (as in the following example "Zits"). The

three sample stories, "Zits," "Gloves," and "Name-calling," are drawn from student writings in fifth grade classrooms which were part of the 1993-94 pilot study which produced this teaching guide. Feel free to use these sample stories as additional role plays in the activity.

Story One: Zits

I feel bullied when people make fun of my zits and how "fat" I am.

Story Two: Gloves

I had just been in Maine, and I had gotten some gloves that I really liked, and I had brought them into school. And this 7th or 8th grader came up to me and asked me "where did you get those gloves?" I asked him why he wanted to know. Then he lifted me up against the wall and asked me again where I had gotten those gloves, and I said Maine. I have been scared of kids in higher grades ever since.

Story Three: Name-calling

One day I went to school and I saw one small girl who was walking in the hall. She was always looking around. Then one tall girl said to the small girl very very very loud, so the other people would hear her, "What are you staring at? The little ant didn't see the human?" Then the little girl looked very sad. Some of the people in the hall heard what the tall girl had said and they started to call the small girl the "ant." Then some more people went in the hall. Some of them called her the "ant." Some of them were laughing and some of them even started to make up some words that mean "little" or "staring." The small girl first ignored it, but in the end she ran to another floor. I think the girl felt terrible, because when she was running down the stairs, some people chased her with their bullying. After school I told my friend about it and she said that it happens usually in school, especially in the halls. I hope that things like that will stop.

Activity

- Divide students into teams of four or five (any "extras" can be bystanders). During the two-day lesson, each team will have the chance to perform one role play for the rest of the class.

- Hand out a copy of a different case study to each student team. Ask each team to choose a "reader" to read the case aloud to the team. Students then discuss the situation and decide who will play the role of bully, target, bystanders, etc. *Option*: to facilitate role-playing, hand out index cards printed with the names of characters involved in each story (teacher, bully, target, older sister, etc.) to each team. **Important Reminder: Do not allow students to act out the bully role where physical contact or intimidation is involved.**

- After teams review and discuss their cases, allow 10-15 minutes for students to rehearse role plays. Ask students to assign a title to their presentation.

- Invite students to supplement a straight reenactment of each scene with one of the following options:

1. The team enacts one or two possible responses by third-party bystanders which would make the situation better.

2. One person on the team assumes the role of an "omniscient narrator" who sets the scene and presents other relevant information about the incident to the audience. S/he can also *read* the bully role in stories where physical contact or intimidation is involved.

OPTIONS	ADVANTAGES	DISADVANTAGES
Change yourself—go on a diet, lose pimples	Can't pick on those features anymore	Hard to do; bully might make fun of something else about me
Ignore the kids—pretend you don't hear, walk away	Bully won't that know s/he hurt my feelings; avoid a fight	They might do it again; might think I'm stuck up
Tell a teacher	Get someone on my side; don't have to deal with bully by myself	Get called a "tattletale"
Agree—say, "it's true"	Turn it into a joke; maybe make friends	Being mean to myself; lose self-respect
Talk to your parents	Get adult advice	Same as telling teacher
Have a friendly conversation with the bully	Maybe bully will realize I'm really a good kid	Might set myself up for another attack

3. Students may use real or imaginary props, costumes, etc.

• Offer to make yourself available as an additional actor in the role plays. **Note:** when teachers perform in role plays, it's often easier for students in the audience to remain objective and serious.

• Remind students that everyone's participation and concentration—the audience's as well as the performers'—is important.

Class Brainstorm and Analysis

• Follow each role play with a class discussion asking students to brainstorm "dilemmas or problems" posed in the scene. For example, students might answer that "the target is scared," "s/he doesn't want to go to school," "two kids ignored the bullying," etc.

• Next, ask students to brainstorm as many ways as possible that the **target** could respond to the bullying. Write students' suggestions, verbatim, under the "Option" heading on the left side of the board or a piece of chart paper.

• Then ask students to consider the advantages and disadvantages of each response. List these to the right of each alternative. See the previous page for a sample of student responses based on the simple role play titled "Zits."

• Conclude by asking students, "If you were in the **target's** shoes, which response would you choose, and why?" Ask students to turn to their nearest neighbor and, in pairs, decide upon the best response. Ask student pairs to explain their choices to the class.

• *Important Note:* After the next role play, ask students to put themselves in the **bystander's** shoes (rather than the target's) and what they

would *actually* do if they saw or overheard someone being picked upon. Then ask the class to brainstorm additional ways that a bystander could intervene in the situation. Write student suggestions, verbatim, under the "Option" heading on the left side of the board or piece of chart paper.

• During this second analysis, deliberately direct conversation to the topic of "courage" and discuss courage from the point of view of a witness to a bullying incident. Once students have examined the advantages and disadvantages of various intervention options, conclude by asking students to consider, again in pairs, "What would be the *courageous* thing to do as a **bystander** if you saw or heard this bullying incident?" Ask student pairs explain their choice to the class.

Homework
Web of Courage
(to follow the first class period of Lesson 3)

• Introduce the webbing activity. Ask each student to write the word "Courage" in the center of a piece of paper and draw a circle around the word. Demonstrate for students on the board or piece of chart paper.

• For homework, ask students to "free associate" and spontaneously generate a wide range of answers to the following question:

"What are the courageous things you can do if you are being bullied, or if you hear or see someone else being bullied—even if you don't like the person?"

• Show students how to draw four or five "strands" around the central word to form the beginning of a "web." Direct students to write their answers at the end of each strand. Students can elaborate by drawing three or four additional "strands" from each answer. Walk students through one strand of a web on the board or piece of chart paper.

Here's an example of a completed web:

- For homework, ask students to finish their webs and then, individually or in pairs, to write a short story, poem or cartoon about one particular "strand of courage."

- Debrief the activity with a class discussion about the various kinds of courage required to stand up for what is right. Alternatively, ask students to act out their writings and personify "courage" for the class.

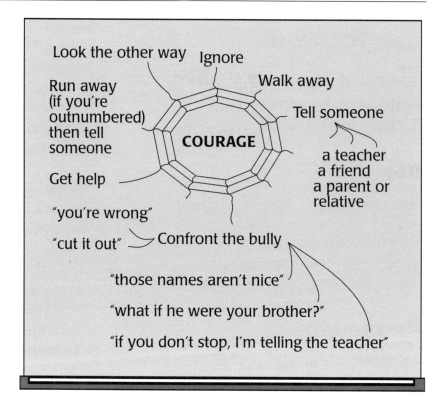

Look the other way   Ignore

Run away (if you're outnumbered) then tell someone

Walk away

Tell someone
a teacher
a friend
a parent or relative

COURAGE

Get help

"you're wrong"

"cut it out" → Confront the bully

"those names aren't nice"

"what if he were your brother?"

"if you don't stop, I'm telling the teacher"

(Second Class Period of Lesson 3)
Possible Discussion Questions

During the second class period devoted to role plays, challenge students to examine the issue of popularity and the double standards that can influence their attitudes and decisions as witnesses. During several of the role plays, designate which characters are friends (e.g., the target and the witness; the witness and the bully) and pose the following questions:

1. When is it easiest to confront a bully or teaser?
2. What kinds of things make it hard to speak out against a bully? What factors determine whether or not you say something?
3. What do popularity and bullying have to do with each other?
4. If you saw someone being bullied, would you think or act differently if s/he were a friend versus someone you don't like or don't know? What's the courageous thing to do?

5. What would you do if the bully were your friend? What's the courageous thing to do?
6. What if the kid who's being bullied has bullied *you* in the past?

Optional Activities

- Art work. Ask each student team to design a poster illustrating what they learned from the role plays and presentations.

- Interior monologues. Ask members of student teams, still working together, to each put themselves into the shoes of a different character in their role play (the bully, target, a bystander). Ask students to imagine what their character might be feeling and thinking during the bullying incident. Then give students five minutes to write an interior monologue or diary entry from their character's perspective. Ask for volunteers representing different characters to read their monologues aloud to the class.

Lesson 4.
Courage by Degrees
Evaluation and Discussion
(1 class session)

Objectives

To evaluate the varying degrees of courage needed to respond to different teasing and bullying incidents; to discuss how the factors of popularity and age influence whether or not and how a bystander intervenes.

Preparation

Students can do this activity individually or in pairs. Each student (or pair of students) needs a pencil and piece of paper to begin.

Activity

• Pose each of the following bullying or teasing scenarios to the class. After each example, ask students to write down the degree of courage they think it would take to intervene on a scale of 1-4, with "1" indicating the least amount of courage and "4" indicating the most. Ask students to write a one- or two-sentence rationale for the degree of courage they think is required in each scenario. Progress quickly through the list.

• "How much courage does it take to...?"

1. Tell one of your friends to stop teasing a kid you don't know very well?
2. Tell one of the popular kids to stop making fun of someone you don't know very well?
3. Tell a bully to stop picking on a kid you don't like?
4. Stick up for your best friend?
5. Step in if a kid who doesn't like you is targeted by a bully?

6. Tell a bully to stop teasing a kid who has bullied *you* in the past?
7. Tell a bully to stop picking on someone who doesn't have many friends?
8. Tell someone to stop bullying if *you* are very popular?
9. Include a new girl or boy in a game?
10. Confront a group of bullies who are pushing a kid around?
11. Confront a bully who is your age and teasing a younger kid?
12. Tell your parents or a relative about someone who is bullying you?
13. Tell your teacher about someone who is bullying you?
14. Tell your teacher about someone who is bullying another student?
15. Tell an older kid to stop saying mean things to someone your age?
16. Ignore someone who teases you while you are playing?
17. Run away from a bully?
18. Run away if you're outnumbered by a group of bullies?
19. Say something to a girl who is picking on a boy?
20. Say something to a boy who is picking on a girl?

Debriefing

After you have read all of the scenarios aloud to the class, discuss with students the different degrees of courage it takes to stand up for oneself or someone else in varying contexts. Possible questions to prompt discussion:

1. Which situation(s), in your opinion, requires the most courage of all (a "3" or a "4") to intervene? Why is it so hard to act in this case?
2. When is it easiest (a "1" or a "2") to help out someone who's being teased or bullied? How are these situations different from the others?
3. How does popularity influence courage?
4. Does age influence courage? How?
5. Does it matter where a situation takes place (e.g., in public or in private)?
6. What's the most courageous thing you've ever done or seen someone else do for another person who was being teased or bullied?
7. In the situations where it's hardest to intervene, can you think of some things that might make it easier to be courageous?
8. What is it about a bully that gives him/her so much power?

Homework
Personal Principles

- In preparation for the assignment, ask students to look up the word "principle" in the dictionary. Then talk with students about personal rules of behavior and conduct:

   "Some principles and codes of conduct are laid down for us by law; for example, it's not okay to steal someone else's belongings or to cheat on your income taxes. Cheating on a test, though not against the law, is against school rules and honor codes. Other principles we define personally and may be different for each of us. When you're faced with a tough situation or decision, it's very powerful to have personal principles. When you have principles, you don't have to act on your first impulse—or go along with what everyone else is doing. Instead, you can powerfully *choose* how *you* want to respond.

- For homework, ask students to write a statement of their personal principles in relation to bullying. Assign students one or more of the following writing topics. **Note:** question three assumes added meaning after students have read *Bridge to Terabithia*.

   1. Describe your principles (or "rules of thumb") as a witness of a bullying situation. How would you like to respond if you saw someone being bullied?
   2. What are your principles as the target of a bully? How would you like to respond if someone were teasing or bullying you?
   3. When (if ever) is it okay to tease or be a bully?

- The following samples are excerpted from student writing on "personal principles":

   ...I think that everyone should be stood up for. No matter what. But if they're already standing up for themselves, and they're doing good, I say <u>don't</u> interfere. Anyway, if it's someone popular, they might have someone else on their side. And if they say something and you don't know what to say back, you're in deep trouble.

   ...If you are the one being bullied, don't feel hesitant to tell a teacher. And even if the bully calls you a tattletale, don't listen because they are probably trying to keep you from telling.

   ...As an observer, I think the best thing to do most of the time is to confront the bullies. You <u>should</u> do that no matter whether you hate the victim or the bully/bullies are your best friends. Of course, it is easiest just to leave [the situation] alone which I have done once or twice.

Lesson 5.
Get the Picture
Cartoon Design and Discussion
(1 class session)

Objectives

To encourage creative, proactive responses to teasing and bullying by third party bystanders.

Preparation

- Photocopy the following handout, "Get the Picture" (p. 23) for student pairs.

Activity

- Ask students to work in pairs.

- Distribute the handout, paper and pencils, crayons, or other colorful art supplies to student pairs.

- Read the sample cartoon aloud with the class and point out the courage it takes for a by-stander to intervene when they see someone being bullied. Ask student pairs to determine a good title for the cartoon and to depict in the third, remaining panel another intervention by a bystander: "If you were standing right next to someone being teased or bullied like this, what is another way you could help them out?" Ask for volunteers to read their cartoon aloud.

- Next ask student pairs to design their own three-panel cartoon. After students have divided a blank piece of paper into three large boxes, ask them to depict in the *first box* only an incident of teasing or bullying that occurs in school or at a school activity.

- Reassure students that they do not have to be a daVinci to do this activity. Stick figures work just fine:

  "Will a boy or a girl be the bully's target? What happens and where? How will the reader be able to tell from your cartoon that this is teasing or bullying, and not just fooling around? What words, gestures or physical interactions are involved? Include conversation or thoughts in 'bubbles' if you like. What is the title of your cartoon? Write this above the three panels."

- Ask a student to demonstrate and draw on the board a cartoon character speaking, and then thinking.

- When student pairs have finished the first panel and have titled the cartoon, collect the papers and redistribute randomly.

- In the second and third panels, ask student pairs to depict two different ways that bystanders could respond to *better* the situation for the target.

- As students present their scenarios, ask the class to suggest additional positive ways bystanders could intervene.

- Collect and arrange cartoons in a special class book; display cartoons around the room; or ask students to submit cartoons to the school newspaper.

Get The Picture

Lesson 6.
"Sticks and Stones"

Class Discussion and Webbing Activity
(1-2 class sessions)

Objectives

To brainstorm courageous steps one can take "after the fact" of a bullying incident; to understand the meaning of "sexist" behavior; to consider the terms "tomboy" and "sissy," as well as the different cultural expectations for girls and boys.

Teaching Note

If students have read *Bridge To Terabithia*, you can ask them to draw parallels between the two stories. In "Sticks and Stones," Jeremy chooses sports and his male friends over a girl; in *Bridge To Terabithia*, Jess remains loyal to his female friend Leslie—and he is teased.

Preparation

Photocopy the following story "Sticks and Stones" (pp. 27-28) for student groups.

Activity

• Ask students to join in groups of two or three, and hand out one copy of the story "Sticks and Stones" to each group.

• Read the story aloud with the class.

• Ask students to put themselves in Jeremy's shoes and, in their groups, to brainstorm and write down answers to the question posed by Jeremy's mother in the story:

"Put yourselves in Jeremy's place. You're feeling so awful about what happened with Ali that you can't fall asleep. Your mother's question keeps spinning through your head, 'What can I do about it?' You decide to get up out of bed and write down a list of all the possible things you could do or say to feel better about yourself..."

• Ask student groups to report their possible "next steps" to the class; compile a list on the board.

• The following class discussion and webbing activity are opportunities to introduce the terms "sexism," "sissy" and "tomboy" into the class vocabulary.

Possible Discussion Questions

1. What would be the courageous thing to do if you were Jeremy in the story?
2. Why is Ali left out of the baseball game?
3. Does anyone know what the word "sexism" means?
4. How many examples of sexist behavior can you find in this story? (List examples on the board.)
5. Do you agree or disagree (show of hands): when a boy picks on a girl, his behavior is always "sexist."
6. What's a good definition of the word "sissy"? Can girls and boys both be sissies?
7. What do we call a girl who acts "like a boy"?
8. Which is worse: to be called a "tomboy" if you are a girl, or to be called a "sissy" if you are a boy?
9. Is there a name for girls that has the same (negative) meaning that the term "sissy" has for boys?

Webbing Activity

- Ask students to draw a circle in the center of a piece of paper and to write the word "sissy" in the middle. Demonstrate on the board or a piece of chart paper how to draw "strands" around the circle to form the beginning of a web.

- Ask students to spontaneously think of as many answers as they can to the following question and to write their answers at the end of each strand of their web:

  "What words would you use to describe a sissy? What is a sissy like? You might write down what a sissy looks like or sounds like... You might write down colors or feelings you associate with sissies. Write down whatever comes immediately into your mind...'

- Repeat the activity substituting the word "tomboy" for "sissy."

- Encourage students to incorporate ideas from their two webs in the homework assignment which follows.

Homework
Tomboys and Sissies

Op-ed Piece and Informal Interview

Objectives

To perceive and analyze the different social norms for boys and girls; to learn from other people's opinions.

Assignment

- Ask students to copy the following question on the top of a page and to write a one-page response for homework:

  "In your opinion, why is it more acceptable to be a 'tomboy' than a 'sissy'?"

- Encourage students to glean ideas from their "Sissy" and "Tomboy" webs, and to use as many real-life examples as possible to support their opinions.

- Instruct students to pose the same question to *two* other people—perhaps an older sibling, relative or next-door neighbor—after students have written down their own opinions. During the two informal "interviews," students should jot down notes on their "interviewees'" responses.

Debriefing: Student Discussion

- Ask students to briefly recap their interview experiences with one another in pairs. This will give each student a chance to speak and to review his/her notes before entering the larger class discussion. Students can take turns asking each other the following questions (which can be written on the board):

  "Who did you interview?"
  "What were their opinions?"
  "Did anything they said surprise you?"

- After pairs have finished, ask students to join in a general class discussion.

Possible Discussion Questions

1. If someone calls you a "tomboy," is this an insult? What's your own opinion?
2. Who did you interview and what did they think about tomboys?
3. Did anyone say something that really surprised you?
4. Who gets teased more often: tomboys or sissies? Why? What's your own opinion?

5. Is it okay for a boy to leave a group of boys to play with girls? What usually happens?
6. What usually happens when a girl leaves a group of girls to play with boys?
7. Is the different treatment given to tomboys and sissies fair? What do you think?
8. Can you think of three things to do that will help make it easier for each of us—whether a girl or a boy—to be our own unique selves?

Samples of Student Writing

The following three responses to the "Tomboys and Sissies" homework assignment are drawn from the writings of a class of fifth graders who participated in the piloting of **Bullyproof** activities in 1993-94:

I think it is acceptable to be a "tomboy" and not a "sissy" in a kid's life because boys (at least some of them) think that being a sissy means acting like a "girly-girl," prissy and stuck-up and not wanting to get your clothes dirty. Since some boys have this athletic, masculine view of themselves, they think it's bad if you're not doing sports all the time. Girls really have a much different opinion of what being a sissy is though. Personally, I think being a sissy means being a wimp—someone who is scared of doing easy things. I think that it is very rude to girls if boys think that being a sissy means you act like a girl. This is a big put-down because it means that girls aren't good enough, so if you act like a girl, it's bad.

I think society allows girls to be tomboys and not boys to be sissies because if not now, then for many generations, boys were more highly prized than girls, so it's all right to become better than yourself, but you can't become worse.

In our society it's thought of as "good" to be brave or adventurous. "Tomboy" means to be adventurous or, in stereotype, like a boy. Therefore, it's all right to be tomboy-ish. But "sissy" means just about the opposite. "Sissy" means non-athletic, possibly helpless. This is the opposite of what society likes. Therefore, it's not all right to be called "sissy." I'm not sure I agree with that. After all, what's wrong with being non-athletic?

Sticks and Stones*

Jeremy and Adam were becoming best friends. It was something Jeremy had always wished would happen. After all, Adam was good at everything he did. He received the highest grades in school, won all the races in gym, and told the funniest stories. It had been so hard getting close to Adam—he just did so many things and had so many friends. But Jeremy had done it!

Ali, another student in the class, had been friends with Jeremy for many years. They were next-door neighbors and their families spent a lot of time together. Ali was good at sports and she and Jeremy would play together almost every day—that is, until Adam entered the picture. Since Adam and Jeremy became friendly, Ali was left out of all their games. You see, Adam didn't like playing with girls. He said they weren't good enough at sports. So, Jeremy went along with him—he didn't want to make Adam mad.

One day, some boys in the class were organizing a baseball game during recess. Ali wanted to play. She liked baseball and was a terrific batter. But Adam said no—he wouldn't play if a girl played. All the boys backed Adam, even Jeremy.

Ali was very mad. She looked at Jeremy and said, "Jeremy, you know I can catch and hit the ball better than most of the boys here!"

Jeremy first looked at Ali, then back at Adam. Adam had a defiant look on his face. Jeremy knew if he disagreed with Adam, that would be the end of their friendship. So, Jeremy yelled back at Ali, "Girls are sissies. You're too little and weak to play with the boys."

* Reprinted from Explore by Jay Cerlo, ©1983, with permission from United Educational Services, Buffalo, NY.

Ali was furious. She stomped away and refused to speak with Jeremy for the rest of the day. Jeremy felt guilty. He didn't really mean what he had said, but he didn't want to look bad in front of the other boys, especially Adam.

That night, Jeremy was very quiet. He ate his dinner quickly, and then disappeared into his room. A short time later, his door opened and his mother walked in. "Hey, buddy," she said, "is something bothering you?"

Jeremy looked at this mother for a few seconds. Hesitantly, he began relating the story about the baseball game. His mother listened patiently.

When Jeremy was done, his mother said, "So you feel crummy about what you did."

"Yeah," replied Jeremy.

"How do you think Ali felt?" she asked.

"Really angry...maybe hurt," Jeremy said.

"Why?" asked his mother.

"Well, probably because I called her some names," he said.

"When you call people names, what are you doing?" she asked.

"I'm trying to hurt their feelings. I know I can hurt their feelings by picking on something that makes them different from others." Jeremy appeared to be surprised at the words that were coming out of his mouth.

"That's right," said his mother. "We pick on people's differences or weaknesses to hurt their feelings. Now that you've succeeded in hurting Ali's feelings, what can you do about it? You know once the words come out of your mouth, you can't take them back."

Jeremy knew his mother was right but he didn't know what he could do to make things better. He sat on his bed with a blank look on his face.

After a few minutes, his mother said, "Think about it, Jeremy, and we'll talk more later." With that, she walked quietly out of his room. Jeremy was left alone thinking, "Sticks and stones may break my bones, and names DO hurt me."

Bullyproof © 1996 Wellesley College Center for Research on Women

Lesson 7.
Real Dilemmas
Class Discussion and Case Studies
(2-6 class sessions)

Objectives

To sort through the complexities involved in real-life cases of bullying and sexual harassment; to try on the roles and respond from the perspectives of various people involved in actual cases; to determine responsibility in these cases; to introduce students to the term "sexual harassment."

Preparation

- Photocopy "One Mother's Dilemma" (pp. 32-33) for all students. This first case will be reviewed by the class as a whole. Students will review the next five case studies in small teams. Decide whether each student team will review the same case, or whether you will distribute a different case study to each team. Photocopy "The Playground," "The Bus Ride," "Badgered By Boys," "Rites of Passage" and "Mooing and More" (pp. 34-42) for student teams accordingly. To help keep students focused, make enough copies so that each student can have his/her own copy of the team case study.

- *Important Note:* All six cases are based on real situations. The behaviors in "The Playground," "The Bus Ride," "Badgered By Boys," "Rites of Passage" and "Mooing and More" may be construed as sexual harassment and might entitle one to file a Title IX law suit in federal court and/or a complaint with the Office for Civil Rights (OCR) of the U.S. Department of Education, the federal agency that has jurisdiction for the enforcement of Title IX (which outlaws sex discrimination in educational institutions). However, when you initially review these cases with young students, it works best to stay within the pre-established, familiar framework of "teasing and bullying"—unless a student raises the issue of sexual harassment himself or herself. Sexual harassment is introduced at the end of the activity and reviewed in detail in Lesson 7, "What Are Your Rights?"

Case One: One Mother's Dilemma

- Hand out and read aloud with the class the first case study, "One Mother's Dilemma." Pause after each scene to pose questions in a general class discussion. Encourage students to provide solid rationale for their answers.

- *Important Note:* Students may wonder why the case continues to escalate after they have made suggestions to better the situation. If this occurs, explain that students can assume that Lucy's mother does not make the same choices.

- During the 1993-1994 piloting of **Bullyproof**, fifth-grade students suggested the following ways to resolve the "mother's dilemma":

Find a different day care center
Have a big conversation with kids and moms and all teachers
Mom goes to school with daughter and talks to the boy
Girl should stand up to boy herself to show she isn't helpless
Mom should get proof
Girl's parents talk to boy's parents
Hear boy's side of the story; he could be an abused child copying adult behavior

Case Two: The Playground

- *Background Teaching Notes:* "Friday Flip-up Day" is a weekly occurrence at many elementary schools. Some school administrators have acknowledged the existence of this activity, but they often have not considered such "child's play" a problem, let alone sexual harassment. Consequently, they have seen no reason to intervene or to punish the perpetrators. Adult silence has amounted to a condonation; the gendered terrorism on the playground has become normalized and expected behavior.*

- Divide the class into teams of four or five students. Hand out copies of the case to students on each team. Ask each team to choose a "reader" to read the case aloud, and a "recorder" to write down team answers to the questions on the back of his or her page. Give students permission to talk and brainstorm aloud about the case.

- After teams have finished analyzing the case, ask designated "reporters" to summarize team answers for the class. Take note of student responses on the board.

Case Three: The Bus Ride

- *Background Teaching Notes:* This case is based on the actual experience of Cheltzie Hentz who, at age six, was the youngest child to file and win a sexual harassment case in Eden Prairie, MN. Both the Office for Civil Rights and the Minnesota Department of Human Rights ruled that the behaviors (carried out on the bus, on school grounds, and in the classroom by boys ranging in age from 6 to 13) constituted sexual harassment.

- Ask students to read the case aloud in their teams and together brainstorm answers to the questions.

- After teams have finished analyzing the case, ask designated "reporters" to summarize team answers for the class. Record student responses on the board.

- During the piloting of **Bullyproof** activities, fifth graders compiled the following list of "courageous things to do on the bus":

Sit or stand next to the girl being teased to protect her
Tell the boys to stop
Sit next to the boy who is teasing and then lean over and interfere
Tell the principal
Organize a group of kids to stop it
Write a letter to the superintendent
Call the boys' parents
Move the boys off the bus
Get counseling for the boys
Put the boys in a special class to help them with their problem
Make a small scene
Try not to embarrass the girl who is being harassed

Case Four: Badgered By Boys

- *Background Teaching Notes:* This case is based on the actual experience of Jonathan Harms, a Minnesota third grader who was harassed by other boys at school for several months in 1993. Initially, in June of 1993, the Office for Civil Rights found "no indication that [Jonathan] was singled out for harassment because of his sex." In September of 1994, the Minnesota Department of Human Rights found "probable cause" in the Harms' case and decided to investigate the claim as sexual harassment under Minnesota state law. The next month, OCR announced it would reopen its investigation.

- Ask the team "reader" to read the case aloud to the student team. Team members together brainstorm answers to the questions. A "recorder" should take notes on the team answers on the back of his or her paper.

---

* *Secrets in Public: Sexual Harassment in Public (and Private) Schools* (1993) by Nan Stein, Working Paper #256, Wellesley College for Research on Women, pp. 4-5.

- After teams have finished analyzing the case, ask designated "reporters" to summarize team answers for the class. Record student responses on the board.

Case Five: Rites of Passage

- *Background Teaching Notes:* Boys are often forced to endure rituals or "rites of passage" as part of an initiation onto a sports team or into a new grade. Some elementary students report being terrified to advance to middle school because they'll have to suffer the rite of passage known as "swirling": older students plunge new students' heads into flushing toilets. Other students must endure being "paddled" by older students upon their transition to a new school. In some states, hazing is a criminal offense and carries a fine, even upon those who have knowledge of the hazing yet have not reported it to the proper state authorities. In other states, hazing is not considered a criminal act. But, in any event, do we want these public performances of violence and intimidation happening in our schools— seemingly under the approving eyes of adults?

  In 1994, the U.S. Federal District Court in Utah refused to allow the locker room incident described in this case study as an actionable case of hostile environment and sexual harassment. The lawsuit was dismissed on the grounds that the boy failed to prove that he had been a victim of any concerted discriminatory effort. However, if this incident had been directed at a female, most likely it would have been viewed as sexual harassment, and there would also have been criminal assault charges pending against the perpetrators. *

- Before students begin the case study, ask them to define the term "rite of passage" and to list common rites of passage that they know about or have experienced.

- Ask the team "reader" to read the case aloud to the student team, and team members to brainstorm answers to the questions. A "recorder" should take notes on the team's answers on the back of his or her paper.

- After teams have finished analyzing the case, ask designated "reporters" to summarize team answers for the class. Record student responses on the board.

Case Six: Mooing and More

- *Background Teaching Notes:* For the purpose of this case study, the sex of the perpetrators has been changed. In the actual case, which took place in Petaluma, CA in the mid-1980's, an 8th grade girl was repeatedly taunted by boys. OCR found the school district in violation of federal law Title IX.

- Divide the class into teams of four or five students. Hand out copies of the case to students on each team. Ask each team to choose a "reader" to read the case aloud, and a "recorder" to write down team answers to the questions on the back of his or her page. Give students permission to talk and brainstorm aloud about the case.

- After teams have finished analyzing the case, ask designated "reporters" to summarize team answers for the class. Take note of student responses on the board.

- After discussion of the six case studies, inform students that the teasing and bullying in five of the cases, "The Playground," "The Bus Ride," "Badgered By Boys," "Rites of Passage" and "Mooing and More," are also considered "sexual harassment." Students will learn more about sexual harassment in the next lesson.

---

* "Sexual Harassment in School: The Public Performance of Gendered Violence" by Nan Stein in *The Harvard Educational Review* 65, no. 2 (Summer 1995), pp. 155-156.

ONE MOTHER'S DILEMMA

Part I.

It is late September. The leaves are turning red and gold, and four-year-old Lucy has just begun her second year at the local child care center. One afternoon during the drive home from school, Lucy tells her mother that a new boy, Brian, hits her almost every day. "Do you ever hit him first?" asks Lucy's mother. "Never," says Lucy. Lucy's mom is furious; her heart pounds and her hands begin to sweat. She knows that the school has a "no-hitting" policy, but it obviously isn't protecting her daughter. She isn't sure what to do.

Questions

What do you think Lucy's mom should do?

What would you recommend Lucy do?

Part II.

Lucy's mother isn't sure what to think. Maybe Brian is temporarily upset because he's new in school, and he'll calm down after a few days. But maybe Brian is always mean and angry and his hitting will continue. Lucy's mom decides to wait a while and see what happens.

One week later, Lucy leaves school with a bruise on her forehead. "Brian punched me again," Lucy reports. "What do you do when Brian hits you?" her mother asks. "I tell him to stop," says Lucy, "and if he doesn't, I walk away and go to the teachers for help." Lucy's mom decides to take action. She visits Lucy's teachers at the child care center and directs them to step in immediately whenever Brian hits her daughter. She calls Brian's parents, explains the situation, and asks them to have a talk with their son. She encourages Lucy to keep speaking up for herself every time Brian bothers her.

But Brian continues to hit Lucy, even though he is sent to the director's office when he does. Lucy's mom senses that the school's "no-hitting" policy contains a double-standard.

Questions

What might be some reasons why Brian continues to hit Lucy?

What is a "double-standard"? Who loses out in this situation?

What is a "dilemma"? Can anyone explain the dilemma in this story?

What do you think Lucy's mother should do now?

If you were Lucy, what would you do?

Continued...

Bullyproof © 1996 Wellesley College Center for Research on Women

HANDOUT

Part III.

Lucy's mother soon realizes that words don't seem to be enough to stop Brian from punching. So Lucy's mom decides to teach her daughter how to fight back. "No one has the right to hit you," she tells Lucy, "but there are people in the world who hurt others and you need to know how to protect yourself!" "But Mom, we're not supposed to hit at school," Lucy insists. Lucy's mother carefully explains that Lucy has every right to defend herself if she's being hurt. Lucy learns how to throw a hard, accurate punch. She practices on pillows and on her mother's stomach.

Questions

Do you think the mother made a good decision? Why or why not?

What else could she have done?

If you were Lucy's mother, how would you explain your decision to the staff at school?

When, if ever, is it okay to break school rules?

aim FOR the center, Lucy

Based on the article "Teaching My Daughter To Fight," by Margaret Dean Daiss, in *Ms.* 3, no.6 (May-June 1993), pp. 94-95.

THE PLAYGROUND

Every Friday was known as "Friday Flip-Up Day" in the elementary school. Any girls who wore skirts or dresses on Fridays would be fair game to have their clothes flipped up by the boys on the playground during recess. "Flip-Up Day" was well-known to parents, teachers and kids alike. It had become a kind of school tradition that had never been questioned or challenged by any of the adults.

Girls tried to remind each other to wear pants on Fridays; anyone who forgot and wore a dress by accident would ask her teachers if she might be excused from the playground, or if she could sit out recess in the principal's office. Other girls would beg to make a telephone call to their parents to see if a pair of pants could be rushed to school in time.

One fall, "Friday Flip-Up Day" was transformed into "Pinch the Private Parts of the Girls Week." Boys chased girls around the playground, grabbing and pinching them, while shouting vulgar comments about the girls' bodies. Some of the girls' parents, outraged at this new form of playground terrorism, demanded that the school principal stop these activities.

Questions

List all of the bystanders in this situation and describe what each could have done differently to make it better for the girls on the playground.

If you were a girl being targeted on the playground, how might you respond?

If you were an older brother or sister coming to pick up your younger sister at school and saw her being chased, "flipped" and grabbed by the boys, what would you do or say?

You don't like what happens on the playground, but several of the boys involved in "Flip-up Day" are your friends. What do you tell them? What would you say to the girls?

From *Flirting or Hurting? A Teacher's Guide on Student-to-Student Sexual Harassment in Schools* (p. 48). ©1994 National Education Association and Wellesley College Center for Research on Women.

THE BUS RIDE

Seven-year-old Pauline took the bus to school every morning, along with lots of other elementary and middle school students from her neighborhood. During the 30-minute ride, Pauline liked to sit and talk with her second-grade classmate Sarah. One morning when Sarah stayed home sick, Pauline sat alone. Two 13-year-old boys got on the bus and sat down in the seat behind her. Halfway to school, the boys started barking like dogs. Pauline giggled, finding it silly to hear animal noises coming from older boys. Her laughter was abruptly cut short: "Hey, stupid," taunted a male voice from behind the seat, "this is what you are." Pauline stopped breathing. She could hear the frightened pounding of her heart.

The two boys continued barking for the rest of the bus ride to school. Several younger boys joined in, adding comments about sex and parts of Pauline's body. Pauline recognized some of the boys from her class, but she felt too outnumbered and too scared to tell them to stop. Although Pauline wasn't sure what all of the words meant, she knew that some of them were bad. She closed her eyes and wished that Sarah were there to hold her hand—or that the bus driver, clearly within earshot, would tell the group of boys to quiet down. But the driver didn't pay any attention.

Pauline was a nervous wreck for the whole day. She was scared to be alone in class and in the hallways. She cried during recess. And Pauline was so worried about the bus ride home, she couldn't concentrate on her school work.

Based on a true account summarized in "Sexual Harassment in School: The Public Performance of Gendered Violence" by Nan Stein in *The Harvard Educational Review* 65, no. 2 (Summer 1995), pp. 153-154.

Questions

If you were also on the bus and overheard the boys, what would be the courageous thing(s) to do? Write down a list.

What could the bus driver do or say that would make a difference?

Because Pauline is so much younger than some of the boys, does she have to endure their behavior?

What are Pauline's options?

You are Pauline's mom or dad. Pauline starts crying when you put her to bed that night. You ask her what's wrong and she explains what happened on the bus. What do you say and do in response?

BADGERED BY BOYS

Part I.

Jonathan loved to play baseball, tell jokes and pal around with his friends, like most eight-year-old boys. In the middle of the school year in third grade, several boys in Jonathan's class started saying mean things to him during the day. "Sissy!" two boys taunted in the lunchroom. "Scaredy-cat!" three other boys jeered at him in the hall the next morning. Later in the week, a crowd of seven or eight boys followed Jonathan home, saying more nasty things than before: "Betcha like to do it with animals!" Jonathan didn't know what the boys were talking about, nor why in the world he had become the prized target of their cruel jokes.

Questions

If you were in Jonathan's shoes, what could you do?

You are a friend of Jonathan's and he tells you what's been going on. What are some ways you could help him out?

Part II.

Jonathan picked at his food at the dinner table. His parents noticed that he was acting oddly and asked Jonathan if something was bothering him. He told them about the other boys in his class. "Would you like us to talk to your teacher?" asked Jonathan's dad. "No, not yet," said Jonathan, "I'll talk to her first." Jonathan arrived at school earlier than usual the next morning and told his teacher about the incidents. "I'm sure the boys are just joking around with you, Jonathan," the teacher said, "Try to lighten up a little."

Jonathan decided to take matters into his own hands. He figured out the perfect way to get his teacher to take him seriously. Jonathan borrowed a small tape recorder from his mom's office and hid it inside his jacket. Over the next few weeks, whenever boys teased or badgered him at school, Jonathan captured their voices and exact words on tape. But when Jonathan and his parents replayed the tape for the school principal, he dismissed the findings. "Don't worry about it," said the principal, "This is normal, everyday play. Boys will be boys! What do you expect?"

Questions

Why do you think Jonathan wanted to talk to his teacher by himself?

If Jonathan had been a girl, do you think the teacher or the principal would have responded differently? Why or why not?

What are some better ways the teacher and principal could have responded to Jonathan?

What does the phrase "boys will be boys" mean? Is it fair?

What do you recommend Jonathan and his parents do next?

Part III.

One afternoon during recess, a pack of boys cornered Jonathan in the schoolyard and shoved him against a tree. Jonathan's book bag fell to the ground as three boys pinned Jonathan's arms behind his back. The terrified boy tried to kick himself free, but couldn't overpower the group who had him surrounded. Two boys jumped on top of Jonathan's feet, anchoring him to the ground and crushing his toes. While other students watched, the boys yanked Jonathan's pants and underwear down below his knees. Then the bullies ran off, laughing, leaving Jonathan alone and humiliated in the schoolyard.

Questions

Suppose you were one of the other students in the schoolyard who saw the group of boys cornering Jonathan against the tree. What could you do or say to help Jonathan?

What could an adult do or say, and at what points, that would make a difference?

Why might some boys behave in these ways toward other boys?

Based on a true account summarized in "Sexual Harassment in School: The Public Performance of Gendered Violence" by Nan Stein in *The Harvard Educational Review* 65, no. 2 (Summer 1995), pp. 157-158.

RITES OF PASSAGE

Part I.

Bursting with joy, Sam ran all the way home from school to tell his mom and dad that he'd been moved from second- to first-string quarterback of the Eagles, the high school's freshman football team. Fourteen years old, Sam had been striving towards this day for months. Throughout his summer vacation Sam had held to a rigorous training schedule, spending four hours each day sprinting on the track and lifting weights in the local YMCA. Never before had Sam devoted so much energy to something he wanted. He couldn't believe that all of his sweat and stamina had actually paid off.

Sam played an outstanding opening game, leading the Eagles to a 21-0 win. No fumbles, no interceptions, no penalties. Sam's arm seemed made of gold. After the victory, Sam was toweling himself dry in the locker room when four of his teammates grabbed his arms and legs and hoisted him onto their shoulders. Sam shouted in surprise and half-expected to be dumped back into a cold shower. But instead, the four boys rammed the quarterback up against a shower pole and, with athletic tape, painfully bound his naked body to the cold metal. Terrified, Sam begged his friends to stop, "Cut it out, guys. This isn't funny!" Other team members gathered around and cheered. "Hey, calm down, dude!" urged Sam's friend Jerris, "This fun is part of the game—welcome to the team!" To conclude the savage rite of passage, several boys dragged a girl into the locker room and forced her to view the taped and naked freshman. Sam hung his head in shame. He tried his best to choke back tears.

Questions

Jerris calls the ritual "fun." Do you think he is right?

If you were a team member in the locker room, what are some courageous actions you could take to help Sam ?

Part II.

The next day, Sam's parents went with Sam to the principal's office to complain. It turned out that the principal and other school officials were already familiar with the locker room episode. "There's nothing I can do," said the principal, "This is part of every second stringer's initiation onto the team." Sam's coach wasn't understanding either. "This is a time-honored tradition," he told Sam. "Dozens of boys have gone through the same thing and survived. There's no need to raise a fuss." After making Sam apologize to his teammates for drawing them negative attention, the football coach kicked Sam off the team.

Questions

List all of the people who are responsible for what happened to Sam in the locker room.

If a girl had been in Sam's position, do you think the principal would have responded any differently? Why or why not?

The coach tells Sam that "there's no need to make a fuss." Do you agree or disagree? Why?

What can Sam do next?

If you knew about this "tradition" in advance, would it keep you from trying out for and/or joining the football team? Why or why not?

Are there any "traditions" among students in your school that you don't like or think are unfair?

Based on a true account summarized in "Sexual Harassment in School: The Public Performance of Gendered Violence" by Nan Stein in *The Harvard Educational Review* 65, no. 2 (Summer 1995), pp. 155-156.

MOOING AND MORE

Part I.

Alyssa's body was developing faster than any of her friends' in the fifth grade. Alyssa was definitely beginning to look like a young woman instead of a girl. In fact, people often mistakenly assumed that Alyssa was a 7th or 8th grader, although actually she had just turned 11.

Surprisingly, the fifth-grade girls gave Alyssa a harder time about her body than the boys. When Alyssa ran to first base during the kickball game, a group of girls on the sideline started "mooing" like cows. The boys snickered. During lunch period and on the bus ride to and from school, girls passed Alyssa mean notes: "How many times do you need to get milked during the day?... Do they make training bras in your size?" A group of girls started trailing Alyssa through the halls between classes, mooing loudly enough for everyone to hear.

Questions

How do you think Alyssa feels?

Put yourself in Alyssa's place. What could you do to get the girls to stop teasing you?

You overhear what's being said to Alyssa on the playground and in the hallways. What would be the courageous thing(s) to do to help her out?

Part II.

One day Alyssa decided to talk to some of the girls and ask them to stop. "I can't help it that my body is changing," she reasoned, "please leave me alone." The girls refused to look Alyssa in the eye; they just laughed and stared at her chest. Alyssa felt like a freak. No one saw and heard her for who she really was anymore. She wished she could crawl into a cave and hide.

Alyssa decided to ignore the girls. Maybe they would stop taunting her if she didn't show any reaction to their jeers. She was wrong. Alyssa clutched her books to her chest when she walked through the halls, trying to conceal her body from the world. But the teasing continued. Finally Alyssa decided to tell her older sister Kirsten what was happening. Kirsten was in 9th grade and would know what to do in situations like this. "Why don't you get a teacher to help you out?" Kirsten suggested. "I'm scared the girls will do something even worse if I tell," said Alyssa, "Besides, why should I trust the teachers? They already see what's going on and don't do anything about it!"

Questions

Do you think Alyssa should follow her sister's advice? Why or why not?

How could a teacher or another adult in the school help out in this situation?

What do you suggest Alyssa do next?

Why might some girls behave in these ways toward other girls?

Based on a true account summarized in *Secrets in Public: Sexual Harassment in Public (and Private) Schools* (1993) by Nan Stein, Working Paper #256, Wellesley College Center for Research on Women, pp. 15-18.

Lesson 8.
What are Your Rights?
Review and Discussion of Sexual Harassment and Relevant Laws
(1-2 class sessions)

Objectives

To define sexual harassment and student's legal rights; to review school policy and procedures on sexual harassment; to review possible ways for targets of sexual harassment to respond.

Preparation

• For your own information, review the two "Background Teaching Notes" (pp. 46-48) on laws regarding sexual harassment in schools, and on the rationale and merits of sending a letter to the harasser. Do not read either of these background notes to students!

• Photocopy and distribute the student handout "Sexual Harassment: It's No Joke!" (p. 45).

• Before class, find out whether or not the school has policies and procedures on sexual harassment for students and adults (teachers, administrators, secretaries, custodians, bus drivers, et al.). Arrange for the principal or a school counselor to visit your classroom and discuss these policies, even if they are unwritten.

• If you have acquired a classroom set of *Tune In To Your Rights*, hand out guides to students and include the "Optional Continuation" section in the lesson.

Discussion: Defining Sexual Harassment

• Ask students to read aloud the "Sexual Harassment..." handout and, as they read along, to circle words they do not understand and underline words they think are key to each point.

Review each paragraph carefully, helping students define any difficult words.

• Inform students of the etymology of the word "harassment." In old English the verb "to harass" literally meant "to set a dog on someone." Thus, the viciousness and power aspects of sexual harassment are inherent in the word's origin.

• Remind students that they already know about five specific cases of sexual harassment: the case studies reviewed in the previous lesson. Point out that girls and boys both get harassed, by members of both the same and the opposite sex.

• Once students understand a working definition of sexual harassment, the next step is to discuss what someone can do if s/he feels they are being sexually harassed in school. Begin by asking students to write down on a piece of paper the names of three people they trust and who would believe them if they were sexually harassed.

A Guest Appearance

• Continue the lesson with a guest visit by the principal or school counselor who will discuss with students the school policies and procedures on sexual harassment. (Review student handbooks, if available and if policies are written in a parlance that students can understand.)

• *Optional Follow-Up Steps:* If the school does not have a policy on sexual harassment, help the class to draft a letter to the local school board stating the need for clear policies and procedures. Students can also schedule time on the agenda of an upcoming school board meeting to inform the larger community about sexual harassment in school and what they think needs to be done in response.

Optional Continuation: Review of *Tune In To Your Rights*

• If you have acquired a classroom set of *Tune In To Your Rights*, ask students to take turns reading aloud select pages from the guide. The following pages are essential reading: **Pages 2-3, 8-11, 14-18**. Include additional pages as you deem appropriate.

• Ask for seven student volunteers to read aloud one paragraph each of "Michelle's Journal" on **Pages 2 and 3** of *Tune In To Your Rights*. Then pose the following questions, one at a time, to the class. After each question, allow students several minutes to brainstorm answers on paper with a partner or in small groups.

   1. Is this sexual harassment? Why or why not?
   2. How does Ken's behavior make Michelle feel? Write down a list of her feelings...
   3. Put yourself in Ken's place. What is he thinking?
   4. If you were in Michelle's shoes, what could you do next?

• After debriefing the first two questions with the class, ask students to read aloud **Page 8** of *Tune In To Your Rights*. After students discuss their own ideas about Ken's thoughts and motivations, review **Page 9**. After students discuss Michelle's options, review **Pages 10 and 11**.

• Ask students, as a class, to discuss what they've learned about the role of bystanders in teasing and bullying incidents. Then direct students, again in pairs or small groups, to write down five things that a bystander could do or say that

would help Michelle in this case. Invite student volunteers to roleplay their responses as bystanders for the class. After discussing and/or viewing student suggestions, review **Pages 14 and 15** of *Tune In To Your Rights*.

• Select seven students, ideally those who haven't yet had the chance to speak up during the lesson, to read Michelle's final journal entries on **Pages 16 and 18**. Carefully review the "Letter to the Harasser" on **Page 17**.

• *Important Points to Review with Students:* In order to send a letter to the harasser, the target must know the harasser and/or be able to identify him or her. The letter is always written with and delivered to the harasser by an adult who has been trained in using this technique. Letter writing is *never required* of the target; it is one *option* s/he can consider. Targets of harassment are not responsible for ending harassment (thus being re-victimized)—school administrators are responsible!

Sexual Harassment: It's No Joke!

- **Sexual harassment is unwanted and unwelcomed sexual behavior** which interferes with your right to get an education or to participate in school activities. In school, sexual harassment may result from someone's words, gestures or actions (of a sexual nature) that make you feel uncomfortable, embarrassed, offended, demeaned, frightened, helpless or threatened. If you are the target of sexual harassment, it may be very scary to go to school or hard to concentrate on your school work.

- **Sexual harassment can happen once, several times, or on a daily basis.**

- **Sexual harassment can happen any time and anywhere** in school—in hallways or the lunchroom, on the playground or the bus, at dances or on field trips.

- **Sexual harassment can happen to anyone!** Girls and boys both get sexually harassed by other students in school.

- **Agreement isn't needed.** The target of sexual harassment and the harasser do not have to agree about what is happening; sexual harassment is defined by the girl or boy who is targeted. The harasser may tell you that he or she is only joking, but if their words, gestures or actions (of a sexual nature) are making you uncomfortable or afraid, then you're being sexually harassed. You do not have to get others, either your friends, teachers or school officials, to agree with you.

- **No one has the right to sexually harass another person!** School officials are legally responsible to guarantee that all students, you included, can learn in a safe environment which is free from sexual harassment and sex discrimination. If you are being sexually harassed, your student rights are being violated. Find an adult you trust and tell them what's happening, so that something can be done to stop the harassment.

- **Examples of sexual harassment in school:**

    - touching, pinching, and grabbing body parts
    - being cornered
    - sending sexual notes or pictures
    - writing sexual graffiti on desks, bathroom walls or buildings.
    - making suggestive or sexual gestures, looks, jokes, or verbal comments
      (including "mooing," "barking" and other noises)
    - spreading sexual rumors or making sexual propositions
    - pulling off someone's clothes
    - pulling off your own clothes
    - being forced to kiss someone or do something sexual
    - attempted rape and rape

Remember:
Sexual Harassment is Serious and Against the Law!

Originally appeared as "Stop Sexual Harassment in Schools," by Nan Stein in *USA Today* (May 18, 1993): 11A.

BACKGROUND TEACHING NOTES
Laws Regarding Sexual Harassment in Schools

Sexual harassment in public schools is a form of sex discrimination, and therefore is prohibited by federal and state laws. Title IX of the Federal Education Amendments of 1972 (20 U.S.C. 1681) states, "No person in the United States shall, on the basis of sex, be excluded from participation in, be denied the benefits of, or be subjected to discrimination under any education program or activity receiving federal financial assistance." In addition, many states have their own laws about sex discrimination and sexual harassment in education.

Sexual harassment is defined as unwanted and unwelcomed behavior of a sexual nature. All legal definitions of sexual harassment enable the recipient (i.e., target/victim) of the behaviors to define whether the attention is unwanted and unwelcomed. This subjective component is built into the Equal Employment Opportunity Commission (1980) and the Office for Civil Rights (1981) definitions of sexual harassment, as well as into state laws and executive orders issued by governors. The presence or absence of sexual harassment thus depends on the target/victim's perception of "unwelcomed" sexual behavior.

Sexual harassment can cover a range of behaviors, including sexual insults and name-calling; off color jokes; intimidation by words or actions; offensive touching such as tickling, pinching, patting or grabbing; pressure for sexual activity; assault; and rape. Harassment may be perpetuated by peers, school staff, or others with whom the target must interact in order to fulfill school or job duties. In schools, sexual harassment may be student to student, staff to student, student to staff, or staff to staff. While both females and males may be the targets of sexual harassment, in the majority of cases the target is female and the harasser is male.

An important point to remember is that sexual harassment is defined by the target. What may be hostile, humiliating, or sexually offensive to one student may not be perceived that way by another student. Therefore, when a target complains about being sexually harassed, it should not be within the purview of school staff members to decide whether or not the situation being described constitutes sexual harassment.

When the specter or hint of a sexually-tinged physical relationship between a minor and an adult in a school setting emerges, sexual harassment has entered a new domain, that of child abuse and criminal felonious behavior. In these cases, sexual harassment may also constitute allegations of child sexual abuse if the harassment involves physical contact of a sexual nature between adults and minors. School administrators, teachers, and other school staff must fulfill their statutory duties as "mandated reporters" and are required by their state's law to report the suspected child abuse to the appropriate state agency, police or district attorney.

In school, sexual harassment can affect a student's academic progress, extra-curricular involvement, social relationships and self-confidence. Sexual harassment in schools that is allowed to occur unchecked can also create a school climate detrimental to the learning environment for all students. In these schools, students may not feel safe or valued as a member of the school community. Such a climate can lead to more serious sexual harassment offenses.

In February 1992, the U.S. Supreme Court issued an unanimous 9-0 decision in the _Franklin v. Gwinnett County (GA) Public Schools_ case. This decision strengthened Title IX by permitting damage awards to individual targets of sex discrimination and sexual harassment. Currently there are other cases at both the district and circuit court levels that will set precedents about school district and individual school staff liability for peer-to-peer sexual harassment.

From _Flirting or Hurting? A Teacher's Guide on Student-to-Student Sexual Harassment in Schools_ (pp. 39-40). ©1994 National Education Association and Wellesley College Center for Research on Women.

BACKGROUND TEACHING NOTES
Sending a Letter to the Harasser/Bully

Writing a letter to the harasser/bully is a step toward taking some control over situations that often cause depression, fear, bewilderment, anxiety and anger in the target of sexual harassment. Thus, the act of letter writing is positive and even therapeutic because it is proactive.

Unfortunately, sending a letter to the harasser/bully does not mitigate the negative collective learning that has already occurred among the bystanders who witnessed or heard about the sexual harassment incident. For that reason this letter writing should in no way be seen as a strategy to prevent or eliminate sexual harassment in general; it will not take the place of strategies such as training programs, support groups, discipline codes and grievance procedures.

Letter writing is not a good option in certain cases, such as when the harasser/bully is a teacher; or, if a student peer, the harasser/bully is particularly anti-social or emotionally disturbed. This strategy should be restricted to first-time incidents of verbal or written sexual harassment.

Letter writing is an *option* for the target—she or he should decide if this is a tactic to pursue. School personnel should not require the target to write a letter. Additionally, in order to send a letter to the harasser/bully, the target must know the perpetrator and/or be able to identify him or her.

Several assumptions underlie the rationale of sending a letter to the harasser/bully:

1. It is an active response to the sexual harassment by the target.

2. It changes the balance of power: the target of the sexual harassment becomes proactive and the harasser/bully is placed in a "receiver" role.

3. It shows the perpetrator there are consequences to these behaviors that live beyond the time of the incident.

4. It catches the harasser/bully alone. The letter should be given to the perpetrator by the target (if she or he chooses) *in the presence of an adult staff member*, preferably in the privacy of the adult staff member's office. If the target would prefer not to be present, then the alleged harasser/bully should be handed the letter in private by the adult.

5. The letter forces the harasser/bully to face up to the behaviors in an adult's office – a different context from the one in which the harassment was committed.

6. It allows the target to feel safe; the perpetrator is confronted, yet not in a face-to-face situation.

7. The letter serves a legal purpose by documenting the incident, the specific behaviors, the presence of witnesses, and the target's feelings. It also serves to give the harasser/bully "fair warning" to stop.

8. It helps to contain the incident of sexual harassment among a small group of people—the target, the adult advocate, and the alleged perpetrator.

The letter is usually written in three parts. The first part includes a statement of the dates and facts: "This is what I think happened..."

Portions of background notes taken from "No Laughing Matter: Sexual Harassment in K-12 Schools," by Nan Stein, in *Transforming A Rape Culture*, edited by Buchwald, Fletcher and Roth (Milkweed Editions, Minneapolis, MN; October 1993). Based on "Dealing with Sexual Harassment," by Mary P. Rowe, *Harvard Business Review* 59, no. 3 (May-June 1981), pp. 42-46.

The second part should describe the target's feelings, and what damage s/he thinks has been done. Appropriate statements in this section include opinions, feelings, anxieties, and worries, such as: "Your action made me feel terrible;" "I am scared that I'm going to be blamed for your behavior;" and "You have caused me to ask for a transfer (drop out of class)."

The third and final part of the letter should contain a short statement of what the target would like to have happen next. Statements such as these would be appropriate here: "I want those behaviors of yours to stop because they make me feel awful, and they interfere with my concentration in class and with my homework ... my grades have been falling."

Lesson 9.
Letter to a Harasser or Bully
Review and Writing Assignment
(1 class session)

Objectives

To give students an opportunity to practice a possible way to respond if they are targets of sexual harassment.

Preparation

• Review the preceding "Background Teaching Notes" (pp. 47-48) describing the technique of sending a letter to the harasser/bully. Do not read this aloud to students!

• Photocopy the following "Sample Letter To the Harasser/Bully" (pp. 51-52) for students.

Preliminary Discussion

• Distribute copies of the sample letter to the class. Point out that this letter is based on the case "Mooing and More" that was studied in Lesson 7. In the case study, Alyssa was tormented by a group of girls. The sample letter is addressed to one of the girls in particular. In actuality, Alyssa would write a letter to each of the girls who had harassed/bullied her.

• Explain to students that writing a letter to the harasser/bully (another student) is one effective way to respond after an incident of sexual harassment or bullying. It may discourage escalation of the behavior

• Ask for student volunteers to read paragraphs of the sample letter aloud. Option: set up three chairs in front of the class, ask two students to pretend to be Alyssa and Samantha (in the letter), and you pose as the adult advocate.

• Review with students the three distinct sections of the letter to a harasser/bully. (If students have copies of *Tune In To Your Rights*, ask them to identify these sections in the letter on **Page 17**.)

"The letter is usually written in three parts. The first part includes a statement of the dates and facts: 'This is what I think happened...' The second part should describe the target's feelings, and what damage s/he thinks has been done. In this section you write down your opinions, feelings, anxieties or worries, such as, 'Your words made me feel terrible,' or 'I'm scared to speak up in class because of your teasing.' The last part of the letter should contain a short statement of what the target would like to have happen next. You might write, for example, 'I want you to stop kicking me because it makes me feel awful and I can't concentrate in class...'"

Homework
In Plain Words

• Ask students, individually or in pairs, to write their own letter to the harasser/bully from the perspective of either Pauline or Jonathan, targets of sexual harassment who were discussed in the case studies "The Bus Ride" and "Badgered By Boys" in Lesson 6. Ask for student volunteers to recap Pauline's and Jonathan's situations for the class.

• For the purpose of this letter-writing assignment, ask students to assume that both Pauline and Jonathan were targeted by one specific person named "Brad."

Debriefing: Role Play (next day)

- Select several representative letters for each case.

- Ask for student volunteers to play the roles of Brad and Pauline. Arrange three chairs in the front of the room and stage a mock meeting in which an adult advocate reads aloud the "Letter to the Harasser" to Brad. The teacher should play the advocate or "complaint manager" and, after reading the letter, ask "Brad" 1) if he understands the problem; and 2) whether he will do what Pauline asks. Repeat the mock meeting for the Jonathan Harms' case.

Possible discussion questions:

1. Do you think this letter will make a difference? Why?
2. Who does the letter help?
3. Suppose that you were the target of bullying or sexual harassment; how could writing a letter like this help you?

SAMPLE LETTER TO THE HARASSER/BULLY

Dear Samantha,

I am writing to let you know how it's been to be in fifth grade with you for the past few months—some of the things that happened between us, how it felt to be in school and on the bus with you, and what I want to happen from now on.

When I think back to the beginning of all this, I remember a few things:

1) At the beginning of the school year in September, you started mooing at me during recess and kickball games.

2) The next few weeks, you passed me mean notes making fun of my body.

3) One day, you splashed milk on me in the lunchroom and teased me about "milking time."

4) During the week of Halloween, I decided I couldn't take it anymore and asked you to please leave me alone. You laughed at me and wouldn't look me in the eye. You pretended you didn't hear me and stared at my chest the whole time.

5) Even when I tried to ignore you this past week, you followed me in the halls, sat behind me on the school bus, and mooed.

Just to write these things down makes me feel sad and mad. On many days I would go home and cry. I don't think you know how much you've bothered me, and how rotten your words make me feel. I'm like you, Samantha—I'm a fifth-grade girl who goes to school, plays with her friends, and has feelings. I'd like you to think about how you'd feel if your sister or your best friend told you that someone said and did to her the things you've done to me. I'm sure you wouldn't feel very good—I don't feel very good about it either.

So, here's how I'd like you to change. First, I'd like you to treat me with respect, as a normal, regular person. Second, stop daring other girls to tease me, since they do what you say. Third, I want you to stop mooing at me, following me, sending me notes, and interfering with my work.

I hope maybe things will change now that you know how I feel.

Alyssa

cc: J. Smith, Guidance Office

Based on a letter written by Nan Stein which appeared in *Who's Hurt and Who's Liable: Sexual Harassment in Massachusetts Schools*, edited by Stein (Massachusetts Department of Education, 1982/1986); and in "No Laughing Matter: Sexual Harassment in Schools" by Nan Stein in <u>Transforming A Rape Culture</u>. edited by Buchwald, Fletcher and Roth (Milkweed Editions, Minneapolis, MN; 1993).

Lesson 10.
Action Alert!
A Brainstorm and Action Planning (ongoing activity)

Objectives

To discuss strategies and actions students can take as a class to eliminate teasing and bullying in school; to explore what it means to be an activist and to respond proactively when a situation needs righting.

Brainstorm

• Encourage students to see themselves as activists, people who take action (often collectively) to change conditions for the better.

> "You now know how to recognize teasing and bullying and ways you can respond as a target or bystander. Now, I'd like us to think about actions that we can take *as a class* to help end teasing and bullying in our school. Each one of you can be a powerful activist! And by joining together, we'll have even more power to make a positive difference and involve a lot of other people, too. Does anyone know or can anyone guess what the word 'activist' means?..."

• Ask students to brainstorm answers to the question, "What can we do to end teasing and bullying in our school?" Encourage students to be as creative (and impractical) as they like.

• List students' ideas on the board or on a sheet of newsprint. If students become stumped, ask them some leading questions; e.g.:

> 1. What groups of people do you need to influence and/or involve as allies to reach your goal? (e.g., teachers, parents, younger or older students).

> 2. How could you manage to make it seem "uncool/stupid" to pick on younger kids in school?
> 3. What are ways you might convince the principal to take teasing and bullying more seriously?
> 4. How could you get your parents involved?
> 5. Can anyone think of ways to use the arts—painting, song, drama—to help put an end to teasing and bullying?

• After students have exhausted their ideas, ask them to gather in groups of three or four to decide upon and discuss *three* actions they think are best and that would create the most change for the better in school. Ask each group to designate a "secretary," who will write down the three choices, and a "spokesperson," who will explain the selected actions to the class.

• Ask spokespersons to report group endorsements to the class, explaining why they think these three particular actions are best. Star the most popular choices on the board.

Action Planning

• Action is only effective if taken! After the class as a whole has decided upon three action steps, ask students if they are willing to commit to following through on one or more actions.

• Discuss the importance of careful preparation, and help students determine what preliminary steps are needed before their chosen action(s) can be set in motion. These might include the following:

1. Talk to the art teacher about using materials to create a poster.

2. Send a memo to teachers of lower grades and find out if they'd allow a student group to perform skits on teasing and bullying for younger students.

3. Find out the submission deadline for news articles in the school paper.

4. Find out the date of the next faculty meeting and request time on the agenda.

5. Find out the dates of school board meetings, and call to request a time on the agenda.

- Help students determine deadlines for their preliminary steps and "timelines for action."

Lesson 11.
Letter to a Friend
In-class Writing and Discussion
(1 class session)

Objectives

To recapitulate and reinforce what has been learned during the unit on teasing and bullying.

Activity

• Ask each student, working on his or her own, to write a letter to a friend about teasing, bullying and sexual harassment. Ask each student to think of an actual friend their age who goes to a different school or lives in another town. (If they cannot think of anyone, students may write to an imaginary person who is struggling with a bully or a harasser at school.)

"At this point, you know more than a lot of people about teasing, bullying and sexual harassment. This knowledge is power: now you can help others learn what to do in these situations. What do you think it's *most important* for someone your age to know about teasing, bullying and sexual harass-ment? What would you advise a friend to do about these things? Have you noticed any difference in yourself or in our class since we began these discussions and activities? If so, tell your friend about these changes and give some examples. And if not, why not?"

• Write the preceding questions on the board for students to use as reference points as they write their letters.

• If students don't know how to properly format a letter, sketch a blueprint on the board delineating a letter's opening ("salutation"), body and closing.

• Ask students to conclude their letters with a postscript, "P.S. Please write back!", and to include their return address.

• After students have finished their letters, ask them to join in groups of three and take turns reading their letters aloud. Instruct each group to choose one representative to read his/her letter aloud to the rest of the class.

• After group representatives have read their letters to the class, continue with a general discussion. Possible questions:

1. How many of you have noticed a difference in yourself since we've been taking an honest look at teasing and bullying? (show of hands) How have you changed?
2. Has anyone noticed other ways that the class as a whole has changed?
3. A bully can't be stopped. Do you agree or disagree?
4. If your little sister or brother were being picked on by a bully, what's the first thing you would tell them?
5. What are the best pieces of advice you would give to a bully?
6. What are the best things you could do to support someone who tells you they've just been teased or bullied?

Optional Continuation

• Help students mail the letters to their friends. Ask each student to bring their friend's exact address, an envelope and a stamp to class by a specified date.

- If necessary, show students how to properly address an envelope. If there is a mailbox near or in the school, schedule time for the entire class to walk to the mailbox so that each student can mail his/her own letter.

- If and as students receive letters in response from their friends, invite them to bring the letters to school and share them with the rest of the class. This is one way to encourage ongoing discussion of the topic.

Samples of Student Writing

The following excerpts are drawn from letters written by a fifth-grade class which participated in the piloting of **Bullyproof** activities in 1993-1994:

Well, since we started this, people in my class and I learned a lot. Now they stopped doing mean things to each other. Like now that people know how I felt when they called me "shrimp" and "shorty" and other mean things, they stopped doing that. Now we don't hurt other people's feelings and respect one another even if the person is short, tall or the opposite sex. (male)

I see a big difference in myself since we started discussing bullying, teasing and sexual harassment. Example: when it was my turn to be captain of the kickball game I picked x as a player. As soon as I picked x, he started to pick all the players and suddenly x was the captain. Not only that but x also picked who was pitcher and the batting order (all stuff a captain does). So, I stood up to x and reminded him that I was captain (I would have never done that before). It made me feel good inside. (female)

I really think sexual harassment can hurt because sometimes people may tease you about your body parts and it really hurts your feelings because you can't change them in any way. It can also interfere with your school work because all your thoughts are on your anger and then you can't concentrate. If I am harassed in the future, I will stand up for my rights and if a teacher doesn't care, I will pressure him or her to punish my harasser. (male)

Why don't you put yourself in the person's place and see how you feel about being bullied and teased. (male)

I do see a difference in the way that all of the boys in the class are treating the girls now. 1) They have mostly stopped teasing us and chasing us down the hallways while we are coming back from recess. 2) The boys have also mostly stopped insulting all of the girls and trying to dis us. I think that the girls have also mostly stopped teasing and bullying all of the shrimpy or short boys. (female)

Ever since [these lessons], I've felt guilty whenever I or somebody else talks about someone behind their backs. I realize that it's no joke and teasing isn't any fun. I think [the lessons] helped us, but all our problems aren't solved. People still talk about other people, but at least now we realize there's a problem. (female)

I used to think sexual harassment was totally irrelevant to my life, and if it should happen it would be very embarrassing if I didn't keep it quiet. But sexual harassment can happen to anyone, and if it does, it's not a secret, you should tell someone. (female)

Resources

Books, Handbooks, and Articles on Bullying

Claire, Hilary. *We Can Stop It! Whole School Approaches to Combat Bullying: A Handbook for Teachers* (London, England: Islington Education Department, 1991).

Doyle, Terrence Webster. *Why Is Everybody Always Picking On Me? A Guide to Handle Bullies* (Middlebury, VT: Atrium Society Publications, 1991). To order, write Atrium Society Publications, P.O. Box 816, Middlebury VT or call 1-800-848-6021.

Keise, C. *Sugar and Spice? Bullying in Single-Sex Schools* (Staffordshire, England: Trentham Books, 1992).

Kutner, Lawrence. "Everybody's Teasing Me." *Parent's Digest*, (Spring/Summer 1994).

Lister, Pamela. "Bullies: The Big New Problem You Must Know About." *Redbook*, (November 1995).

Marano, Hara. "Big. Bad. Bully." *Psychology Today*, (September/October 1995).

Morrisey, Mary. "Even Adults Are Afraid to Take on the Schoolyard Bully." *Counseling Today*, (September 1995).

Olweus, Dan. *Bullying at School: What We Know and What We Can Do* (Oxford: Blackwell, 1993).

Rofes, Eric. "Making Schools Safe for Sissies." *The High School Journal*, (October/November 1993, December/January 1994). Reprinted in *Rethinking Schools* 9 (3), (Spring 1995).

Skinner, Alison, ed. *Bullying: An Annotated Bibliography of Literature and Resources* (Leicester, UK: Youth Work Press, 1992).

Whitney, I. and P.K. Smith, "A Survey of the Nature and Extent of Bullying in the Junior/Middle and Secondary Schools," *Educational Research* 35 (1), (Spring 1993).

The following four books, published in the United Kingdom, can all be ordered through the Countering Bullying Unit, Professional Development Centre, Cardiff Institute of Higher Education, Cyncoed Road, Cardiff, Wales, CF2 6XD. Phone: (0222) 551111; Fax: (0222) 747665.

Tattum, D. and G. Herbert. *Bullying: A Positive Response, Advice for Parents, Governors and Staff in Schools.* (Cardiff, Wales: Cardiff Institute of Higher Education, 1990). This booklet has sold over 100,000 copies. In 1992 it was sent to every school in the United Kingdom.

Tattum, D. and D. Lane, eds. *Bullying in Schools* (Stoke-on-Trent, UK: Trentham Books, 1988). This was the first book on bullying published in the UK.

Tattum, D. and E. Tattum. *Social Education and Personal Development* (London: David Fulton Publishers, 1992). Chapter Six deals with bullying in primary schools.

Tattum, D., ed. *Understanding and Managing Bullying* (Oxford: Heinemann, 1993). This is an international, up-to-date textbook

Miscellaneous Resources on Bullying

Be a Buddy, Not a Bully. A poster available for $7.00 from the Mid-Atlantic Equity Consortium, Inc., 5454 Wisconsin Ave., Suite 1500, Chevy Chase, MD 20815. (301) 657-7741.

Bullying and Victimisation in Schools, a British-sponsored listserv on the Internet. To subscribe, send the following command to "listserv@nic.surfnet.n": "subscribe bully-L <firstname> <lastname>".

Articles on Sexual Harassment

Adler, Jerry. "Must Boys Always Be Boys?" *Newsweek*, (October 19, 1992): 77.

Atkins, Andrea. "Sexual Harassment in School: Is Your Child at Risk?" *Better Homes and Gardens*, (August 1992): 32-34.

Cheevers, Jack. "Juvenile Sex Harassment." *Los Angeles Times*, (July 4, 1995): B1,6.

Colino, Stacy. "Fooling Around or Sexual harassment?" *Parenting*, (June/July 1993): 30.

Goodman, Ellen. "Sexual Bullies." *The Boston Globe*, (June 6, 1993): 73.

Kutner, Lawrence. "Harmless Teasing, or Sexual Harassment?" *The New York Times*, (February 24, 1994): C11.

Lanpher, Katherine "Reading, 'Riting, and 'Rassment." *MS*, (May/June 1992): 90-91.

LeBlanc, Adrian. "Harassment in the Halls." *Seventeen*, (September 1992): 162-165, 170; "Harassment at School: The Truth is Out." *Seventeen*, (May 1993): 134-135.

Saltzman, Amy. "It's Not Just Teasing: Sexual Harassment Starts Young." *U.S. News and World Report*, (December 6, 1993): 73-77.

Stein, Nan. "Sexual Harassment in School: The Public Performance of Gendered Violence." *Harvard Educational Review* 65, no. 2 (Summer 1995), pp. 145-162.

Stein, Nan. "Sexual Harassment: When Bullying Goes Too Far." *Parent's Digest* (Spring/Summer 1994), 35.

Reports, Guides, and Pamphlets on Sexual Harassment

Flirting or Hurting? A Teacher's Guide on Student-to-Student Sexual Harassment in Schools (Grades 6 through 12) Nan Stein and Lisa Sjostrom (1994). Available for $19.95 from the Wellesley College Center for Research on Women, Publications Department, 106 Central Street, Wellesley, MA 02181-8259. (617) 283-2510. Published by The NEA Professional Library.

Hostile Hallways: The AAUW Survey on Sexual Harassment in America's Schools. (1993). Available for $8.95/ 11.95 from the AAUW Sales Office, P.O. Box 251, Annapolis Junction, MD 20701-0251. (800) 225-9998, ext. 246.

Secrets in Public: Sexual Harassment in Our Schools. A report on the results of a *Seventeen* magazine survey by Nan Stein, Nancy L. Marshall, and Linda R. Tropp. (1993). Available for $11.00 from the Wellesley College Center for Research on Women, Publications Department, 106 Central Street, Wellesley, MA 02181-8259. (617) 283-2510.

Secrets in Public: Sexual Harassment in Public (and Private) Schools by Nan Stein. (1993). Working paper #256. Available for $9.00 from the Wellesley College Center for Research on Women, Publications Department, 106 Central Street, Wellesley, MA 02181-8259. (617) 283-2510.

Tune In To Your Rights: A Guide for Teenagers about Turning Off Sexual Harassment. (1985). Available in English, Spanish or Arabic for $4.00 from Programs for Educational Opportunity, School of Education, #1005, University of Michigan, Ann Arbor, MI 48109-1259. (313) 763-9910.

What is Sexual Harassment?; Flirting or Harassment?; Harassment? Don't Take it! Fold out pamphlets available for $32.00 per 100 from ETR Associates, P.O. Box 1830, Santa Cruz, CA 95061-1830. (800) 321-4407.

Books for Children

Carlson, Nancy. *Loud Mouth George and the Sixth Grade Bully* (Minneapolis: Carolrhoda Books, 1983). After having his lunch stolen by a bully twice his size, George and his friend Harriet teach the bully a lesson he'll never forget—by bullying him in return (not necessarily the best strategy to resolve the problem).

Yashima, Taro. *Crow Boy* (New York: Puffin Books, 1955). In a Japanese village, Chibi is teased by his schoolmates because he is shy and different from the rest. A new teacher encourages him to express his talents and his peers appreciate him at last.

Mazer, Norma Fox. *Out of Control*, (New York: Morrow Junior Books, 1993). For older students. After spontaneously sexually harassing a girl named Valerie at school with his two best friends, 16-year-old Rollo finds that his life is changed forever. Captures the dual perspectives of the perpetrator and target of harassment.

Stoltz, Mary. *The Bully of Barkham Street* (New York: Dell, 1963). Sixth grader Marty struggles to shed his long-standing role of neighborhood bully. In the process, he discovers other areas in which he can shine.

Stoltz, Mary. *The Dog on Barkham Street* (New York: HarperCollins, 1960). Sixth grader Marty teases and bullies his next-door neighbor Edward. The story highlights the target's point of view.

Taylor, Mildred. *Roll of Thunder, Hear My Cry* (New York: Bantam Books, 1976). Coming-of-age story of a black girl living in Mississippi during the 1930's. A family grapples with prejudice, discrimination, and intimidation.

Paterson, Katherine. *Bridge To Terabithia* (New York: HarperCollins, 1977). Ten-year-old Jess in rural Virginia has much to learn from Leslie, the unconventional girl who moves to town. During the course of their various adventures, and before Leslie's tragic death, the two friends must decide how to respond to the school bully.

Estes, Elinor. *The 100 Dresses* (New York: Harcourt Brace, 1944). For younger students. A group of girls pick on someone who is a little different. Told from the perspective of the bully's best friend who gives into peer pressure and joins the crowd.

Organizations Working for Equity in Schools

The Bill of Rights Education Project: Works with teachers to make civil liberties and civil rights relevant to students. Runs summer teacher institutes and teacher/student conferences. A free tri-annual newsletter *Bill of Rights Network* available from the Bill of Rights Education Project, 99 Chauncy Street, Suite 310, Boston, MA 02111. (617) 482-3170 x314.

Educators for Social Responsibility (ESR): Develops curricula and trains teachers with a particular focus on conflict resolution. A *Resources for Empowering Children* catalogue available from ESR, 23 Garden Street, Cambridge, MA 02138. (617) 492-1764.

Facing History and Ourselves: Develops curricula and trains teachers to engage adolescents in an examination of racism, bigotry, and anti-Semitism through a study of the Holocaust. Information available from Facing History and Ourselves, 16 Hurd Road, Brookline, MA 02146. (617) 232-1595.

National Coalition of Education Activists (NCEA): A quarterly newsletter *Action for Better Schools* and information available from the National Coalition of Education Activists, P.O. Box 679, Rhinebeck, NY 12572. (914) 876-4580.

Rethinking Schools Ltd.: Publishers of *Rethinking Schools*, a quarterly activist educational journal. Subscription rates $12.50 per year. Available from Rethinking Schools, 1001 E. Keefe Ave., Milwaukee, WI 53212. (414) 964-9646.